BORN REBEL

GROWING UP IN SUNDERLAND
IN THE 1950s AND 1960s

MICHAEL WILLIAMS

First published 2022 by Wrate's Publishing

ISBN 978-1-7396165-1-9

Copyright © Michael Williams, 2022

Edited by Michael Williams.
Typeset by Wrate's Editing Services
www.wrateseditingservices.co.uk

Maps drawn by Michael Williams ©

A CIP catalogue record for this book is available from the British Library.

To
My sister Vanessa

For
My sons David and Henry

In memory of
Pauline Mullen and Graham Mole

CONTENTS

LIST OF ILLUSTRATIONS

All from the author's collection except where indicated.

Cover photograph shows the author aged 6 in 1955. Back cover photograph shows his mother Mary and grandfather James in 1939.

LIST OF MAPS

All maps drawn by author

South Shields 1910–1960

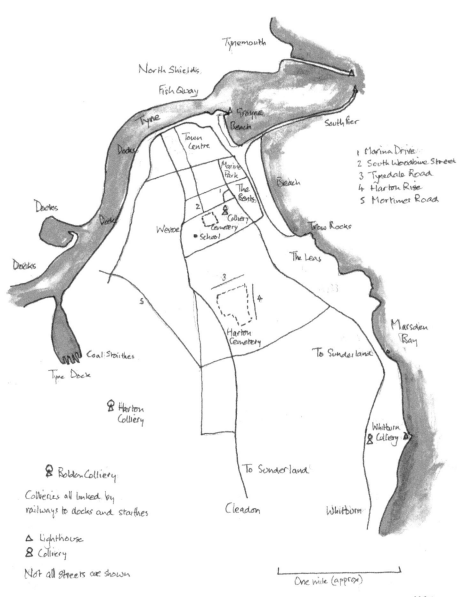

Tynemouth

North Shields

Fish Quay

Tyne

Docks

Town Centre

Marine Park

Groyne Beach

South Pier

1 Marina Drive
2 South Woodbine Street
3 Tynedale Road
4 Harton Rise
5 Mortimer Road

The Parks

Beach

Docks

Docks

Docks

Westoe

Colliery
Cemetery
School

Trow Rocks

The Leas

2

1

3

4

5

Marsden Bay

Harton Cemetery

To Sunderland

Coal Staithes

Tyne Dock

Harton Colliery

Whitburn Colliery

Bolden Colliery

Collieries all linked by
railways to docks and staithes

To Sunderland

△ Lighthouse
⚲ Colliery

Cleadon

Whitburn

Not all streets are shown

One mile (approx)

MJW

ix

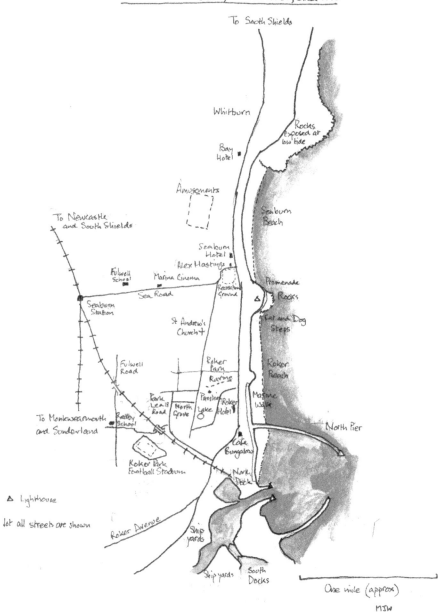

Roker and Seaburn, Sunderland, circa 1955

To South Shields

Whitburn

Bay Hotel

Rocks exposed at low tide

Amusements

To Newcastle and South Shields

Seaburn Beach

Seaburn Hotel

Alex Hastings

Fulwell School

Marina Cinema

Sea Road

Recreation Ground

Promenade

Rocks

Seaburn Station

Cat and Dog Steps

St Andrew's Church +

Roker Beach

Fulwell Road

Roker Park Ravine

Roker Beach

Park Lea/8 Road

Parish Roker Hotel

North Grove

Roker Lake

Marine Walk

To Monkwearmouth and Sunderland

Redby School

Café Bungalow

North Pier

Roker Park Football Stadium

New Dock

△ Lighthouse

Not all streets are shown

Roker Avenue

Ship yards

Ship yards

South Docks

One mile (approx)

MJW

x

Hill View, Sunderland, circa 1960

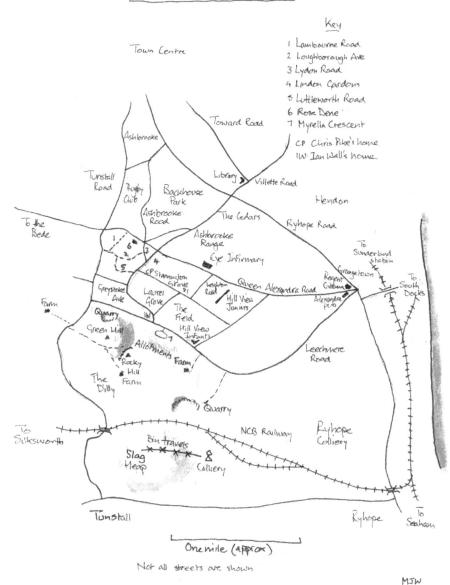

Key

1 Lambourne Road
2 Loughborough Ave
3 Lydon Road
4 Linden Gardens
5 Littleworth Road
6 Rose Dene
7 Myrella Crescent

CP Chris Pike's home
IW Ian Wall's home

Town Centre

Ashbrooke
Toward Road

Tunstall Road
Rugby Club
Backhouse Park
Library
Villette Road
Hendon

To the Bede
Ashbrooke Road
The Cedars
Ryhope Road

Ashbrooke Range
Eye Infirmary
To Sunderland station

1 6 3
4
5
CP Stanningten Grove 91
Leighton Road
Queen Alexandra Road
Grangetown
To South Docks

Greystoke Ave
Laurel Grove
The Field
Hill View Juniors
Regent Cinema
Alexandra pub

Farm
Quarry
IW
Green Hill
Hill View Infants
Leechmere Road

Allotments Farm
Rocky Hill Farm
The Dilly

Quarry

To Silksworth
NCB Railway
Ryhope Colliery

Bin travels
Slag Heap
Colliery

Tunstall
Ryhope
To Seaham

One mile (approx)

Not all streets are shown

MJW

PREFACE

In *The Rainbow* D H Lawrence wrote an epic of ordinary life about three generations of the fictional Brangwen family in his corner of the East Midlands in the late 19th and early 20th centuries. I've dared to attempt something similar for three generations of my own family from the North East of England during the first two-thirds of the 20th century.

Lawrence discovered when writing *Sons and Lovers* that he had to go back to Paul Morel's grandparents to explain relations between Paul and his mother. He did the same with Ursula Brangwen in *The Rainbow*. His wife Frieda probably introduced him to Thomas Mann's *Buddenbrooks* about three generations of German merchants.

My family was no more (or less) special than the fictional Morels and Brangwens. This memoir is based not just on memory but on written and photographic sources – so-called 'ego documents' that give a flavour of individual lives. I have sought to transcend nostalgia and to make a contribution to history which will attract an audience beyond family and friends and people from my generation and my part of England.

I began in strange days, in June 2020, three months into the Covid pandemic, as the nation began to emerge from the first lockdown. I'd read a dozen or so books from the pile I'd accumulated on top of the bookcase behind me. I'd finished marking forty or fifty essays about the growing tension between the United States and China by students on a Master's course at the local business school. I never met them. Teaching went online after the first student at the school fell ill with Covid. I wanted an activity to fill my time as summer loomed, without my regular dancing and swimming, or prospect of holiday.

One of the books I'd read was the third of Ian Mole's memoirs of his childhood and youth in Sunderland where we'd grown up. Ian was five years younger than his brother Graham, my closest friend during my teens. Then Ian had been beneath my notice. My sister Vanessa put us in touch after he published his first volume in 2017, in which Graham features as an overbearing big brother. By then he'd been dead for three years. I often talked to Ian about trying my hand at a memoir. One day he challenged me just to get on with it.

The obvious place to begin was with George Orwell's essay 'Why I Write'. I found that I felt much the same as Orwell, and the words started flowing. Soon I'd hit on a title and a theme. Within a couple of days I'd finished the first chapter. I sent it to Vanessa, on whom I could rely for an honest assessment. She liked it. So did my friend Svetlana in Florida, cut off by travel restrictions. Then I spread the family photograph albums and letters and press cuttings around me and started on the next chapters, about my grandparents and parents.

Initially I planned to cover my life to my early 30s, devoting just one chapter to my childhood. I soon discovered that Ian and Vanessa were right in warning that once I began writing the memories would crowd in and I wouldn't be able to keep within such narrow bounds. Soon I concluded that the right point to finish would be in 1967, aged 18 and about to leave home for the University of Sussex.

I've borrowed two techniques commonly used by historians, by exploring important themes in rough chronological order and beginning each chapter with an episode illustrating my theme. Chapter 5, for example, begins by describing an episode of truancy and goes on to examine the roots of my impulse to rebellion. I follow a similar approach in subsequent chapters.

I spent about a week on each chapter. Once I'd chosen my theme and an opening episode I'd work steadily on each successive chapter. I already knew how I'd finish. In the Epilogue I describe the walk I'd take most days during the spring and summer of 2020. All the time I'd be composing in my head. After dinner I'd write for a couple of hours until the 10.00 pm News. I might resume for an hour or two before bed. Often I'd wake from sleep, recalling episodes that had lain dormant for decades. I'd follow one recollection after another through the labyrinth of memory until sleep overtook me. Memories would pop back into my mind as I composed the following day.

I was consumed by my writing. Once I'd finished a chapter I'd send it to Vanessa and Svetlana. Then I'd take a break for a week. I'd read a book on contemporary British social history. I'd already read David Kynaston's *Austerity Britain* about the Attlee years. Now I read *Family Britain* and *Modernity Britain*, taking the story to 1962, and Juliet Gardiner's "intimate history" of *The Thirties*. Restored and replete with fresh insights, I'd begin the next chapter.

For my teenage years – from 1962 when I turned 13 to 1967 – I drew heavily on my diaries. I transcribed all but the most routine entries into a large notebook. I was able to test my memory against what I'd written. Sometimes the diary confirmed things I'd doubted. Sometimes I found I'd remembered episodes correctly but misplaced in time. Sometimes I uncovered events I'd forgotten. Occasionally I found fragments of conversation. The diary obliged me to confront my young self in the raw – bringing it all back home, so to speak. It allowed no hiding place. It helped me to situate my life in history in a documented account of growing up in the 1960s – and to bring a flavour of Sue Townsend's Adrian Mole to my narrative.

I made enough copies of my first draft to circulate among family and friends. Meanwhile I continued my researches, notably through exchanges with members of Facebook groups with a shared interest in Sunderland and Bede Grammar School which I'd attended between 1960 and 1967. I'd ask if anyone else could recall circus elephants parading through the streets or Breton fishermen wheeling bicycles from door to door with onions strung from the handle-bars, and found that people did. I hadn't been imagining things. I found photographs that revived memories of lost industries. I contacted childhood friends who provided new material and corroborated my recollections. Meanwhile I reread Dominic Sandbrook's account of the "Long Sixties" from 1956 to 1970 in *Never Had It So Good* and *White Heat*. I found a pile of letters from my family when I cleared the garage. All the time I was making notes on my first draft. I resumed work on the book after I resigned from the business school in February 2021. Before long I'd finished a second, expanded version. In September I went back to South Shields and Sunderland to walk the scenes of my childhood before completing a third draft before Christmas.

At last I felt I'd done justice to my material. I'd begun to look for a printer when I learned that I'd attracted enough students at a local adult education centre to run a course on global history in the last phase of the First World War and the turbulent years that followed until the mid 1920s – a period that I'd discovered as a schoolboy and had engrossed my interest since then as the foundation of the modern age. In April I resumed work and made my final revision.

When reading non-fiction narratives I've always wanted to know what the protagonists looked like. I've found myself constantly referring to photographs – or regretting their absence. I've inherited half a dozen albums containing maybe around a thousand photographs. The earliest, from the 1920s, must have been taken with primitive box cameras or folding cameras like one I used as a toy as a boy. Most were taken with the compact cameras containing 35mm print cartridges that became available in the 1930s, used enthusiastically by my mother. I've also inherited a few studio portraits from Edwardian and Victorian times and lots of loose photographs spanning decades. I've included a select few at the head of each chapter and some of them within, along with a few drawn from the web.

I was inspired by two remarkable memoirs – J R Ackerley's *My Father and Myself* (1968) which I re-read after half a century, and Viv Albertine's

To Throw Away Unopened (2018), which seemed to show signs of Ackerley's influence. She might have called it my mother and myself – as I might have called this book my grandfather, my mother and myself. I've sought to write in the same candid spirit.

Michael Williams
June 2022

THE PILGRIM'S PROGRESS

CHRISTIAN'S COMBAT WITH APOLLYON.

Chapter 1
Battling Apollyon

But now in this Valley of Humiliation poor Christian was hard put to it, for he had gone but a little way before he espied a foul fiend coming over the field to meet him; his name is Apollyon. Then did Christian begin to be afraid, and to cast his mind whether to go back, or to stand his ground. But he considered again that he had no armour for his back, and therefore thought that to turn the back to him might give him greater advantage with ease to pierce him with his darts; therefore he resolved to venture, and stand his ground.

(John Bunyan, *The Pilgrim's Progress*, 1678)

Like generations of children before me, the first work of literature I read was Bunyan's *Pilgrim's Progress*. I lingered over the picture of Christian's battle with Apollyon in my father's edition – drawn by Savile Lumley who'd created the famous poster: "Daddy, what did YOU do in the Great War?" We know Bunyan spent a couple of years as a teenage lad in the Parliamentary army in the last phase of the Civil War. We don't know whether he saw battle, but he would have learned how to stand in line in Cromwell's infantry.

I've found no mention of Bunyan in George Orwell's writings, but he too knew how to stand his ground. In a famous essay 'Why I write' (written in 1946) Orwell identified "four great motives for writing". First was egoism, "the desire to seem clever, to be talked about, to be remembered after death", among other things. Yes – guilty as charged. I've always wanted to have my say. I was one of those children who'd pipe up in adult conversation – to my parents' (or at least my mother's) delight and probably to other adults' irritation. Our parents encouraged Vanessa and me to take part in conversation round the dinner table on all manner of topics. My father would tease his wife if she objected to anything especially outrageous. When I was 14 my friend Ian Wall joined us for tea one Saturday. He told me at school on Monday that he'd have been beaten if he'd spoken so freely at table in his own home. I've always thought that said more about his home than mine. I was a keen member of the school debating society and I'd speak up at student union meetings. As a civil servant I'd be liable to throw a verbal grenade to enliven a tedious meeting. I became known as a difficult colleague – and an outspoken one at the business school where I taught for 26 years after quitting government service in 1995.

Orwell's second motive was aesthetic enthusiasm – pleasure "in words and their right arrangement". Guilty again: I've always sought mastery of the written word. I can't recall a time when I haven't found pleasure in composing even the slightest piece of prose. I'm lucky always to have followed professions – as a Whitehall civil servant and university lecturer – that offered a daily opportunity to refine my writing. Orwell's third motive was historical impulse. That's me again. I've always loved history. I've dreamt of playing a part on the great stage. I couldn't resist responding to Boris Johnson's adviser Dominic Cummings' summons in January 2020 to "assorted weirdoes" to apply for jobs as political advisers – in my case as self-styled historical consultant. When Covid struck, I'd have reminded ministers how David Lloyd George responded to the shells shortage in 1915 by forming the Ministry of Munitions to galvanise production – rather as the government created a task force to develop a vaccine against the virus. By giving a wider setting to my childhood and youth and to the lives of my parents and grandparents, I hope in this memoir to make a small contribution to history as well as to enlighten and entertain. Orwell's final motive was political purpose – "desire to push the world in a certain direction". Yes: for me the historical impulse has been inseparable from the political impulse. I wrote to Cummings not from sympathy for the man and his master but from un-slaked appetite for political action, to put my hand upon the wheel of history. I've invoked John Lilburne and John Bunyan in the belief that we can still find inspiration in their examples.

Aged 71 when I began writing I've lived long enough to know the shape of my life. My arrow is curving to the ground, as my near contemporary Richard Thompson writes in a memoir of his early life. Lockdown (and then retirement) provided opportunity for reflection and writing. I know how much I'd have enjoyed reading a similar memoir by my mother or father. I know my sons enjoyed reading the first draft of my own. I've always enjoyed reading published diaries and memoirs. As a research student I read as many working class memoirs from the period of the Industrial Revolution as I could find for an essay about them. Some of my favourite novels have had an autobiographical bent, like *Sons and Lovers* or *Buddenbrooks.* No literary work has had greater impact than Bunyan's *The Pilgrim's Progress.* As a boy I read it as an adventure story like the self-educated working men whose memoirs I'd read. Now I can see it as a call to a strenuous life as well as a Christian allegory and spiritual autobiography. Diaries (especially political ones like Alan Clark's and Tony Benn's) have long been favoured bedtime reading. I own a couple of shelves of autobiographies, from classics like Rousseau's *Confessions* to recent acquisitions like my neighbour Andrew Tarnowski's *The Last Mazurka,* a kind of Polish *Gone with the Wind.* I've had plenty of sources of inspiration.

For a title I did think of "My Life as a Rebel", but that's been taken by the redoubtable Angelica Balabanova for her part in the international socialist movement a hundred years ago. I wouldn't want to provoke comparison. Then I recalled the exclamation "you're a born rebel" by a manager at the business school ten years ago. I'd been delighted by the unintended compliment. I can't recall the occasion but it would have been provoked by some infringement of one of the increasingly onerous rules that have suffocated public services since the 1980s.

I've always chafed under authority. In a phrase from my youth, I've wanted to do my own thing. When I listened to the Crystals' 'He's A Rebel' (released in 1962) I'd imagine they were singing about a boy like me: "See the way he walks down the street / Watch the way he shuffles his feet / My, he holds his head up high / When he goes walking by, he's my guy" – and so it continues. Look out for the recording on YouTube (though it doesn't feature Darlene Love who sings on the record). What strikes me now, and must have struck me all those years ago before I'd even kissed a girl, was how the rebel inspires love: "When he holds my hand I'm so proud… [J]ust because he doesn't do what everybody else does / That's no reason why I can't give him all my love… / That's no reason why we can't share a love". This is no hymn to a bad boy such as Amy Winehouse might have sung: "He's always good to me, good to him I'll try to be / Cause he's not a rebel to me".

Looking back a born rebel was never likely to flourish in the civil service. My hope of becoming a university lecturer was frustrated when I failed to find a post after three years as a research student. My topic was "popular infidelism" – working-class opposition to Christianity in the late 18th and early 19th centuries. I wasn't as engrossed in my research as I ought to have been. In 1973 when my grant ran out I might have gone back to Sunderland to live with my parents while finishing my thesis. Aged 24 I didn't want to return to living under the eyes of my parents. Instead I took a series of jobs – as a comprehensive school teacher in Romford, as a research assistant at Lancaster University, and finally as a clerk in a London University medical school – before winning a place in the fast stream of the civil service in 1974. I felt like Kim Philby after he was recruited by the NKVD: "One does not look twice at the offer of enrolment in an elite force."

One of my contemporaries was Diane Abbott. I came across her in the late 1970s – I assume it was her: I don't suppose there was more than one handsome Black woman in the fast stream then – at a meeting addressed by Enoch Powell at which she stood up and asked a question (I can't remember what about). She'd have gone through the same recruitment process and was probably asked the same questions (perhaps by the same people) as me. Some years ago I heard her say on the radio that one of those questions had been about why she wanted to join the service. She'd said she was attracted by the opportunity to wield power – exactly how I'd answered the same question. It must have been the answer the panel wanted to hear. Of course civil service policy advisers don't wield power directly – ministers decide. But the late 1970s were times when politicians on left and right were claiming that real power was exercised by their nominal servants. *Yes Minister* began to be screened in 1980. It might have been satire, but the plots were inspired by ministerial diaries and memoirs and insider gossip.

A university manager might have called me a born rebel but my father called me a born boss. He didn't mean it as a compliment. There's no contradiction. History is full of revolutionaries who've turned into formidable executives: Cromwell, Washington, Robespierre, Lenin, Stalin, Mao, Castro, Khomeini. The list is long. Opportunity was all. Robespierre probably would have lived out his days as an attorney in Arras if Louis XVI had not summoned the Estates General to meet in 1789. Lenin might have died in exile in Switzerland if Germany had not destroyed Tsardom. I lacked the ambition and dedication to pursue a conventional political career in Parliament. Instead I've come to recognise something of myself in Thomas Gray's famous lines (from his 'Elegy in a Country Churchyard') about "[s]ome village Hampden that with dauntless breast / The little tyrant of his fields withstood; / Some mute inglorious Milton… / Some Cromwell guiltless of his country's blood." Only in imagination have I been (like John Lilburne) one of Cromwell's "russet-coated captains", or a Jacobin tribune during the French Revolution, or a leather-coated Bolshevik commissar like Tom Courtenay's Strelnikov in *Dr Zhivago*.

I've taken pride in combativeness. A tough managing director for whom I worked as company secretary cum finance director in one of my last civil service jobs told me that I didn't just knock a man down in argument; I stamped on him. My MD was a hard-bitten Irish engineer. Once I had to act as formal witness while he reprimanded a senior colleague who'd committed a security lapse. Our chastened colleague walked out of the MD's office, across the room shared by three secretaries and head-first into the door to the corridor, falling on his back stunned to the floor. I was the only person to see the whole episode. I left when much of my job disappeared. I learned later that the MD had sacked the qualified accountant appointed in my place.

As a village Hampden I've had my moments. Aged 6, I took matters into my own hands when my headmistress treated me unfairly. In my early 40s on my way out of the civil service I addressed a mass meeting of members of the Department of the Environment which had been called to oppose relocation to Docklands. That evening my excited mother phoned to tell me I was on the TV News. I caught a glimpse of myself as the "besuited civil servant" whom the *Financial Times* and *The Independent* reported as summoning 400 colleagues to adopt the slogan of the "recalcitrant Vietnam draftees of the late 60s: 'Hell no, we won't go.'" Now my cards were marked. In the late 1990s, after I'd left the service, I led neighbours in a campaign to win compensation for releasing a restrictive covenant and thus allowing a supermarket to be built behind our homes. Our household's share paid for a string of posh family holidays. At the business school I could be relied upon to challenge any silly management initiative. I'd had enough once teaching went on-line.

I must have inherited my combativeness and cussedness. Vanessa has been the same. I recall mothers of local children coming to the door to complain about her bossing their offspring. As a grammar school girl studying for O Levels she would come on like one of the Shangri-Las. For years until she retired as a school manager she was a thorn in the sides of the head teacher and his board of governors. Our mother would claim to be acting in the public interest when she criticised poor service. As a clerk in an earlier incarnation of the Benefits Agency she'd treat claimants as though the funds in her charge were her own money. One evening during my student days my father was thumbing through a thousand pages of William Blake's complete works when he struck on one of 'The Proverbs of Hell': "Always be ready to speak your mind, and a base man will avoid you." My grandfathers were masters of their maritime domains – one striding the bridge like Wotan and the other commanding the engine room like Alberich among the Nibelungs. Like Bunyan's pilgrim I've always been ready to give battle to Apollyon.

Chapter 2
Sailors and Their Wives

PS Give Mike a big hug for me.

(Captain James Williams, writing to Mrs Norah Williams from MV *Ah Kwang*, at Sandakan, North Borneo, 19 March 1950)

I'm Mike. That's me in the top right photograph opposite, on grandpa's knee on the steps of his home in Marina Drive in South Shields in August 1949. He might have been looking at a print when adding his PS. His elder daughter Mary (my mother) probably took the photograph. That's her on his knee in the top left photograph, taken in a studio in 1917, when my mother would have been about the same age as I was in the other photograph. Her mother Norah rests her hand on her husband's shoulder. James Williams was aged 26, in the uniform of Chief Officer in the merchant navy. Norah was 24. They've passed on their taste for elegant footwear to their grandson. My mother had two photographs on her dressing table – one of her father aged around 40 and another of me at 20. The photograph from 1949 must have had special meaning. I've found several prints among photographs inherited from my parents, my aunt Myfanwy and my grandparents.

I was 7 months old when it was taken. I must have preferred Grandpa Jim to Grandma Norah. I'm making a pout as she raises me like a trophy for a photograph which must have been taken on the same day. Two other photographs show me with Grandma Peggie, my father Jack's widowed mother – Big Gran in contrast to Little Gran, for the most obvious of reasons. In one she's steering the Silver Cross pram from which I'm turning to smile at the camera. In another she's looking solemnly at the jolly little boy in her arms. Grandpa Jim was nearly 60 and Little Gran Norah two years younger, though they both look at least 70. Big Gran was 80.

I descend from Welsh sailors and Northumbrian women – strong, spirited folk – who met in South Shields in the late 19th and early 20th centuries. In those days North East England and South Wales were pillars of Britain's coal-mining and shipping industries (the biggest in the world) and not the de-industrialised and impoverished areas they are now. Colliers from Cardiff, Barry and Newport would have put into South Shields. Ambitious young men would have studied at the Marine School for their officer's tickets. Sailors would have met local women in pubs and music-halls and in chapel (rather than church) – or by introduction to shipmates' daughters and sisters. The sea was a dangerous calling: it killed more men than coal mines. A quarter of sailors in the merchant navy in the Second World War lost their lives – a higher proportion than for any of the armed forces. The table of remembrance at the back of St Andrew's in Roker, Sunderland lists nearly as many names from the merchant navy as from the army for the First World War and more than from any fighting service for the Second. Sailors' wives had to be strong and resourceful enough to sustain their families while their husbands were at sea, often for long periods. They had to endure the constant fear that their men might never return, and to bear the burden when they did not.

Seven years separated Jack and Mary but their parents belonged to different generations – and different classes in a finely stratified society. Jack's father David was born in Barry in 1865 and his mother Margaret (always Peggie) in 1872 in Howden village on the north bank of the Tyne opposite Jarrow. David had two brothers and Peggie six siblings. He was a skilled engineer (described in the 1901 census as a steam engine maker/fitter) who followed the sea and ultimately rose to become chief engineer. She'd been in domestic service in South Shields until they married in 1897. The 1911 census lists her as head of a household of six living in South Woodbine Street in South Shields. Ten years earlier the family had been living in a two-storied terrace house in Fairless Street in the town centre. Now they occupied the first floor of a similar house on the edge of town. Jack was the last of five children, born on 30 November 1910 and proud to share a birthday with Winston Churchill (born in 1874).

I'm looking at a studio photograph taken not long after Jack was born. His mother Peggie sits with her children arranged around her. I assume that his father David was at sea – unless he was living apart from the rest of the family, as the census implies. Jack's mother is approaching 40. She's wearing a jacket with padded shoulders and a tie, her long solemn face topped by a wide-brimmed hat capacious enough to contain hair which women wore long in those days. Jack sits on her lap, tightly muffled with only his eyes showing. On her left stands her older daughter Winifred (always Winnie) born in 1898, wearing a wide-brimmed hat pushed back to show a pretty face. In front stands her younger sister Peggie, born in 1906 and wearing a little girl's bonnet. To the right of their mother stand the eldest son David (always Davy) born in 1900 and Sam born in 1902. Jack was the Benjamin of the family, probably an unplanned addition to a crowded (and possibly divided) household.

I've placed another, less formal photograph from 1922 at the head of this chapter because it contains the only surviving portrait of my grandfather David. It was probably taken by one of the family rather than by a studio photographer. They must still have been living in South Woodbine Street where David Williams died. He stands on the left, aged 57 but still handsome, with dark hair slicked back and head inclined towards his wife. He must have spent most of a working lifetime in the engine rooms of steamships. This was a hard world, described vividly by historian John Darwin.

> While engineers looked after the boilers, pipework and drive shafts, 'firemen' and 'trimmers' (sometimes 'stokers') fed the furnaces that heated the boilers. Even in temperate climates this was savagely hot work, at temperatures up to 50 degrees centigrade. Firemen used huge shovels to distribute the coal and pull out 'clinker'. Trimmers broke up the coal in the bunkers using sledgehammers, and brought it in barrows to the furnace. Since coal often exhaled gas, no lights could be used, for fear of

explosion, and the ship's motion threw trimmers and their barrows about in the narrow metal gangways between bunkers and furnace.... These were gruelling, debilitating tasks, for trimmers especially. It was little wonder that firemen and trimmers were four times more likely to commit suicide than other seamen.

This was a world in which a man might raise a thirst.

My father said little about him but I formed an impression that he'd been a distant and possibly oppressive father, fond of a drink and a bet – not a good provider; which might explain why the family never left their pokey flat in South Woodbine Street. I learned from Peggie's granddaughter Ruth that Jack's sister had been just as reticent about their father. My mother recorded in a family album that her father-in-law (whom she could have barely known) liked singing and playing an accordion, as well as a game of cards – obviously a convivial sort, unlike Jack who might well have taken the pledge as a boy and barely touched alcohol until his 60s, on holiday in Spain. My father never raised a hand to me – which suggests he'd felt the weight of his father's hand. Possibly my grandfather had increasing difficulty in finding work following the end of the post-war boom when trade shrank in the early 1920s. He died in 1941, aged 76, a few weeks after my parents' wedding. I'd love to know more about this mysterious man who left barely a trace behind him.

The years seem to have borne more heavily upon Peggie, aged only 50 in 1922 but looking older than her husband. My Big Gran must have been about six foot, dressed usually in sombre clothes – in contrast to Little Gran, standing about five foot, and usually brightly dressed. Peggie seems just as taciturn as in 1910, with a long horse-face, spectacles, and a streak of white hair running back from her forehead – as my father would acquire in middle age. My mother recorded Peggie's interests as family and music, passing on that second interest to her youngest son. She spent her last years living near young Peggie in Manchester and then Lowestoft. I recall visits during the

1950s. I thought her a grim old soul, though I'm sure she was a kind, strong woman. She lived on until 1962, dying aged 90, a relic of Victorian England.

Beside her in the photograph stands young Peggie, aged 16, with a pretty, open, smiling face. She was my father's big sister. They corresponded regularly until he died in 1998. She died the following year, aged 93. My fondest memory is of a visit in May 1964 when she cooked a perfect Baked Alaska, a child's dream pudding, hot sponge surrounding frozen vanilla ice-cream. She probably lived with her parents and younger brother until the mid 1930s when she married Robert Crome, with a nice steady job as an accountant. They had one son, David, born in 1937. The family must have spent some years in South Shields before moving to Manchester where Robert found work. In a letter of condolence following my father's death in 1998 David recalled happy visits and generous gifts from my parents during the war. After his father lost his job the family moved to Lowestoft to run a post office. Robert died in 1964. Peggie survived him by 35 years.

At the front of the 1922 photograph stands my father, aged 11 or 12, with the serious, open, even ingenuous, face that he'd keep for life. Already the family must have been living under the shadow of death. Beside young Peggie stands Sam, 21, natty in his three-piece suit, grinning like one of the Peaky Blinders. Within three years he'd be dead from tuberculosis. Absent from the photograph is Winnie, aged 24 and married. She must have been already sickening from the TB that would kill her within a year or so, depriving two boys of their mother. TB killed people from all classes but mainly from among the poor, living in over-crowded conditions like that top-floor flat in South Woodbine Street where the children must have shared bedrooms. In the 1930s TB killed one in eight people, not many fewer than in Victorian times when it killed one in six. In Jarrow deaths from TB were higher in 1930 than in 1900. TB doesn't kill quickly. People sicken and decline for years. It was known to infect other members in a household. "Consumptives" (sometimes called "lungers") bore the weight of social stigma, shunned by others. By the 1920s care was improving. Sam and Winnie would have had access to a "panel" doctor under the 1911 National Insurance Act. Winnie probably died faster than Sam. She'd have wanted to stay with her husband and sons. I believe one followed the sea and the other preached the gospel. Sam might have lingered two or three years in a specialised sanatorium, in chilly wards open to the elements because fresh air was thought to be good for the lungs. My father was always encouraging me to take "deep breaths" when out for a walk, and to sleep with open windows.

Also absent, probably at sea, is the oldest son Davy, aged 22 – my father's big brother and my favourite uncle. Somehow I've inherited a smart tan saddle-leather toiletry case bearing his initials: D.W. After rising to captain, he spent the Second World War in New York, organising convoys by day and – I like to think – enjoying the bars and clubs of Manhattan by night. By the time I met him in the 1950s he'd risen to commodore in charge of Shell's shore establishments in Britain. In 1953 he found a ship for his brother's father-in-law (my Grandpa Jim) for a final voyage to replenish his savings ahead of retirement. I remember him standing the family slap-up meals in the Roker and Seaburn hotels on the seafront in Sunderland. Always careful with money (like my father) he retired with his wife Mabel to a small bungalow in Eastbourne. I saw him for the last time in July 1970 when he stood dinner for my parents and me at the Old Ship Hotel (of course) on the sea front at Brighton where we were staying for my graduation ceremony from Sussex. A friend took a photograph of my father and uncle and me walking along the front, which I lost when the wallet in which I kept it was stolen a few years later. Davy died suddenly and silently in 1982. He and Mabel were sitting in front of the television one evening. She got up to make a cuppa and returned to find him dead – out like a light. I'm not sure by how many years she survived him.

Some photographs capture moments that look forwards and back across decades. I own three photographs (all taken by different men) of my father's family at Peggie's home in Lowestoft in August 1964. This was the biggest family gathering in my childhood. I've chosen the photograph in which my father (aged 53 and fourth from left) cracks a rare smile caught by a camera.

He had driven from Cromer where the family were spending a couple of weeks in the guest house where my parents had stayed in 1948. Aged 15 I was pre-occupied with my own concerns – mainly girls – but my father must have relished this unique opportunity to meet his surviving brother and sister among their families.

The three of them – my father, Peggie aged 57 and Davy aged 64 (third, fourth and fifth from the left) – stand at the heart of the gathering. Peggie's husband Robert had died a month or two earlier. On the left stands her son (my cousin) David, aged 26. His wife Sandra (aged 21) stands beside me. They'd married the previous year and their first daughter Ruth had been born in July. Vanessa, just short of 12, her face partly hidden by modish hair, stands between David and our mother, aged 47. Beside Davy stands Mabel. Their daughter Audrey stands behind me and Sandra. Audrey's husband Steve Canning must have taken the photograph. The lad in lederhosen is

Nicky, their only son. Davy, Peggie and Jack were notably less fecund than their parents and grandparents.

By 1964 Cousin David had embarked upon a career as a solicitor culminating in his appointment as recorder in 1990. He carried forward the family tradition of Liberalism by standing for Parliament in 1966 and 1970, losing his deposit both times. In 1977 he left the party for the Conservatives as the Jeremy Thorpe scandal unfolded. As an ardent Baptist he'd contemplated missionary service in the South Pacific but stayed in England to support his mother Peggie in her bereavement. He got there in the end, spending two years as the Principal Judicial Officer for the Solomon Islands in the early 1980s. He took a theology degree and led a Baptist congregation in Beccles until death from cancer in 2011. Four hundred mourners attended his funeral. He and Sandra were the most fecund of the family, raising three daughters who've given birth to six children who've already presented Sandra with three great-grandchildren. David set great store by family. I visited with my wife and sons in 2001. I recall book-shelves full of theology. He took us boating on the Waveney. He and Sandra would have liked to entertain us again but my marriage ended soon afterwards. The next time I saw him was while he lay dying, surrounded by his family. Steve and Audrey made lives in Coleraine. We never met again though we'd exchange Christmas cards. Audrey was troubled by schizophrenia and endured spells in hospital. She died in 2008, followed by Steve in 2014. Nicky never married. I sent a message last year but received no reply.

My father's parents David and Peggie were Victorians. They'd seen Britain change into a country in which most people lived in towns and cities, and most men worked in mines and factories. By 1914 South Wales produced more coal, of the best quality, than anywhere else in Britain, with a thriving export trade. North East England built more ships than anywhere in the world. Colliers put into ports serving the coalfield in Northumberland and Durham. David and Peggie were entering mid-life when the old Queen died in 1901 and well into middle age when war broke out in 1914. I've surmised that David probably left the sea when trade contracted in the early 1920s.

My mother's parents James and Norah were a generation younger. They belonged to that most fateful of generations, one that deserves a capital – the Generation of 1914. They were in their early 20s when war broke out. They must have lost friends but they contrived to marry and start a family. They built a good life during the 1920s before the onset of the Depression in 1930 destroyed the global trading system on which Jim's livelihood and his family's comfort and security depended. By the late 1930s he'd gone back to sea but was soon pitched into war again as he approached his 50s. He survived but his health did not. Jim spent the 1940s at sea. In 1950 he bought a small shop that quickly failed. He went back to sea in 1953 for a final voyage to replenish the family savings while Norah disposed of the shop. He spent a few years in retirement before dying aged 67 in 1958 – just as Harold Macmillan was about to proclaim that some of our people had never had it so good. Like my other grandmother, Norah lived on for twenty years after her husband died.

James Williams was born in Swansea in 1890. He bore the same name as his father, born in Aberaeron in 1863, who'd gone to sea and risen to ship's officer by the time his son married in 1916. By family tradition his mother was an illiterate Irish girl. I can follow my grandfather's career from his Continuous Certificate of Discharge which seamen were required to present as they moved from one ship to another. His begins in 1904 when he joined a clipper bound for Australia as a cabin boy. Within months he was reclassified as an ordinary seaman and by 1906 as an able seaman. He'd made third mate by 1911, second mate by 1912, first mate by 1916 (hence those three bands on his cuffs) and master in 1927 – cabin boy to skipper in 23 years. By the time he retired in 1953 he'd spent almost half a century at sea. He voyaged to all parts of the world: the Far East, South America, Russia and the Soviet Union, India and the USA as well as Australia. He kept letters of commendation inside his CCD. One from 1916 describes him as "a most willing and attentive officer and strictly sober". Another from that year describes him as "strictly sober". In 1917 he's described as "reliable, sober & attentive to his duties"; in 1918 as "a good officer, capable and energetic and of sober habits"; in 1920 as "a good navigator and of sober habit"; and finally, in 1921, as "a splendid officer, energetic, strictly sober and always reliable and attentive to his duties". James Williams must have been a rare specimen to be commended so uniformly and so emphatically as sober – in contrast to my other, more stereotypically nautical, grandfather. My mother listed his interests as football, cricket, music, films, drama and musical biography. I'll call him Captain Jim – he'd have appreciated the nod to his favourite author Joseph Conrad.

By 1916 first officer James Williams was in a position to marry my grandmother Norah Caisley Howard – Little Gran. Howard is a familiar English name of Germanic origin. Caisley is common in Northumberland. I have a pair of studio photographs of Norah's Caisley grandparents taken about the time they married in 1859. Her grandfather John's sporting side-whiskers. He's described in his marriage certificate as a police officer. In 1969 Norah made a cutting from the *Shields Gazette* with a story from 1869 about PC Caisley giving evidence against a woman he'd arrested for being "very much the worse for drink and creating a great disturbance. This was her ninth appearance. She was fined 5s. with costs." By family tradition he became a detective. His father had been an agriculturist – presumably a small farmer, a step or two higher than farm labourer. PC Caisley's wife Elizabeth is wearing a crinoline in her photograph, hair gathered in a chignon. Her father was a commercial traveller. I have a studio photograph of their daughter Mary (my mother's grandmother, whom she resembled) taken around 1888 when she married Charles Howard in South Shields. Charles was a coachman, like his father, who eventually established himself as a coal merchant, probably one of many delivering coal from door to door. I'm guessing Charles and Mary must have paid a visit to London in the early 1890s, since I've inherited from their daughter Norah what was probably their copy of the 1892 edition of Baedeker's Guide – invaluable if you're planning a novel set in Sherlock Holmes' London. Theirs was the Northumbrian lower-middle class – more than a cut above the Welsh farm labourers from whom my grandfathers descended.

Norah was born in 1892, second of Charles and Mary Howard's five children, following their son Charles born in 1890, whom the 1911 census lists as a shipyard draughtsman. My mother bore the middle name Franklin after a second son born in 1899 who found work on a bookstall. Theirs was the world of Mr Polly. A third son Albert was born in 1901. He and Franklin both survived service on the Western Front. A daughter Mary was born in 1893 but died three years later. Her father bought the family plot in Harton Cemetery where she was first to be interred. Norah was the only one with progeny. I have a studio photograph taken on her confirmation day, probably around 1905. It shows a pretty, poised young woman displaying a pair of slender ankles below a white dress ending at mid calf. Another studio photograph, possibly taken before the war as a gift for Jim whom she'd already begun seeing, shows her in a light suit, with hat and handbag – and the same slender ankles. You can see she's small – no more than five foot. My mother listed her interests as embroidery and crochet (she was a milliner) and music – but also poetry and politics. She passed on her interest in politics to her daughters and ultimately to her grand-children and their progeny. I have on my shelves a volume of Longfellow's poems with an inscription from Jim dated March 1914. The two of them might have met while he was studying for an officer's ticket at the Marine School in South Shields. Her parents must have welcomed this sober yet convivial and able young man. She was lively, pretty and intelligent.

I've placed the earliest photograph of this pair at the head of the chapter, from the disorderly photograph album which Norah must have compiled in the 1940s. The album contains a playful photograph from the early 1920s showing her at the ship's wheel. She's wearing a cloche hat hiding bobbed hair and an elegant jacket and a skirt ending above her knees. A studio portrait shows her in a flimsy flapper's dress. By the mid 1920s Jim could afford to buy or rent a substantial new detached house in Tynedale Road on the edge of South Shields near Harton Cemetery. Photographs show it standing apart amid fields. Not long afterwards it was demolished to make way for the semi-detached houses that line the street now. My mother told me she grew up in a home with servants. A photograph shows a uniformed maid holding Myfanwy, born in 1924. Twins Ivor and Shirley were born in 1930. Ivor lived until 2019. Shirley died after six weeks and was buried in the family plot.

The 1930s were harder. Jim was unable to find a ship as trade contracted. Jim and Norah had to dispose of the house in South Shields. I'm guessing he would have insured against the loss of work. Anyway he had sufficient reserves to buy a substantial home, a former coaching inn with six bedrooms, in Aberaeron where the family lived until the mid 1930s. They returned to South Shields after Jim found a ship as trade revived in the run-up to war, moving into a substantial new semi-detached house in Marina Drive near the sea-front. The street must have been full of the sounds of ships and pit, with Westoe colliery only a few hundred yards away. By 1938, with Mary working as a junior manager in the local Labour Exchange, the combined earnings of father and daughter were enough to allow Norah and Mary to visit the South of France.

I'm saving the story of Jim's maritime exploits for the next chapter. Thanks to newspaper cuttings preserved by his womenfolk – Norah and daughters Mary and Myfanwy – I can assemble detailed narratives of his part in two rescues in the North Atlantic in the 1920s and his encounter with a U-boat in 1941. Famously Winston Churchill claimed that "[t]he only thing that ever really frightened me during the war was the U-boat peril.... I was even more anxious about this battle [of the Atlantic] than I had been about the glorious air fight called the Battle of Britain." I'll show the qualities that merchant mariners brought to the battle and the dangers they overcame in order to prevail. This was Britain's longest, hardest battle – against Germany's most resourceful and courageous fighting men – and its greatest victory.

Judging by the few letters that have survived, Jim was an assiduous correspondent. In the late 1940s and on into 1950 he captained a tramp steamer working the South China Sea between Malaya and Borneo – Conrad's haunts. The first of his surviving letters, written on 14 January 1948, during the hard times following the Second World War, describes how he'd just despatched two food parcels, which

> should be there some time in February. I think they are improving the selections in the parcels now as the last one has 16 ozs margarine in it. The one I sent from Penang is coming to you from Australia & the following stuff is in the parcel. 1 tin of dried eggs, supposed to be the product of 24 fresh eggs, 1 – 16 oz tin of bacon rashers, 2 – 12 oz tins of luncheon beef, 1 – 16 oz tin of ham & tongue, 1 – 12 oz tin of full cream milk powder, 1 – 2lb tin of honey, 1 – 16 oz tine of dripping. So that's quite a nice assortment.

Another letter, dated 19 March 1950, describes conditions that Conrad would have recognised.

> Of the two I much prefer the Malaya Coast than these parts [North Borneo], there are a tremendous lot of coral reefs and atolls about for to make it a pleasant place to be knocking about. It's bad enough if it's a fine clear day, but as you have read of these very bad tropical showers, they are that heavy & of course then there is nothing to be seen, it's for all the world like a dense fog & of course if they last any length of time & and very frequent. Then you can readily understand that it's then a very risky business to carry on, so the only sensible thing to then is to let go the anchor & stay put.

All this time Jim was suffering from troubles with his feet resulting from nearly two weeks of immersion in the bilge of an open boat after being torpedoed in 1941 – troubles aggravated by tropical heat. He was also worried about Ivor.

I'm making a second exception for another family photograph which arrests the flow of time over decades.

Taken in October 1949, this is the only one showing all three siblings. Ivor, aged 19, sits in front. Myfanwy, aged 25, holds me in her lap. Behind her sits proud Mary, aged 32. Both daughters were settled. Mary had married in 1941. After my father was demobilised from the RAF in 1945 the young couple had bought a house near her parents. My father and Jim both supported Sunderland football team. Jack would keep copies of the *Football Echo* for Mary to include with letters to her father. The lads were already a trial to their supporters, judging from a remark in one of Jim's letters home from his last voyage, in October 1953: "One must admit though considering the money they spent in transfers just before the commencement of this season, they are certainly not setting the Wear on fire with their exploits to date." Myf found work in an office in Birmingham during the war and spent the rest of her life in the city.

Ivor must have been home on leave from national service in the army. His schooling had been disrupted when he was evacuated, aged 9, to

Workington on the Cumberland coast. He seems to have left school in 1944 without qualifications. He might have worked for a year or two as a "Bevin boy" in a coal mine. He seems never to have acquired a trade. After he left the army in 1950 with no obvious prospects his father did what he thought best: he left the sea, sold the house in Marina Drive, and used the proceeds to buy a newsagents' business in Bewdley on the Severn west of Birmingham, with the aim of providing Ivor with some kind of livelihood.

He might have had another reason. As a boy my father used to tell me that Grandpa had another woman in Australia, whom he'd met during those voyages in the South Seas in the late 1940s. I had long dismissed this tale as malicious tittle-tattle until Vanessa told me over lunch one day while I was revising this memoir that he had indeed conducted a liaison in Australia. His wife found out and one day walked fully clothed into the North Sea a few hundred yards from Marina Drive. Fortunately she was rescued. Guilt must have been another reason for leaving the sea. I'm reminded of the way Joe Ackerley discovered after his father's death that he had maintained another family, and how Viv Albertine learned more about her mother's first marriage from papers found after her death. My own parents nursed secrets.

I've no idea why Jim and Norah hit on Bewdley. Perhaps they wanted to be close to Myf in Birmingham; perhaps it seemed to offer a promising business opportunity; or perhaps they wanted to get as far from the sea as they could in England. I visited Bewdley at least once and recall walking to the station with my father to watch the trains. Perhaps this outing prompted me to utter what my mother recorded in April 1951 as my first sentence: "Engine go 'long there". Thanks to Mr Google I can view my grandparents' shop. It's now a gents' hairdresser in the centre of town but the owners have kept the original frontage, which must be much the same as in the 1950s.

The business wasn't a success. By the end of 1953, as Jim neared the end of his last voyage, Norah was trying to sell it. On 18 November he told her how delighted he was to know that at last someone is really interested in that business, if ever I had to go back to that shop, I am very much afraid that I should just about go mad. You will hardly credit how much I loathe & detest that place & Bewdley generally. To me the thought of it is just a nightmare.

The loathsome shop was preying on his mind when he wrote again on 23 November.

> I do sincerely & very fervently hope that you will get rid of it very quickly. As you say it's much easier to buy than to sell, still for all that I hope & trust that you will be lucky & get rid of the place. I am sure that you will be very glad to get rid of it, in fact I am sure you will be more pleased than I will be. You must be fed up with it, what upset me so much was putting all those long hours in & all for nothing. If there had been anything to show for all the hours, I would have been quite prepared to put up with it. To spend all those hours hanging about there from 5.30 to after 7.0 pm & then have to draw on our capital to eke out a living was just more than I could put up with. As you know it was getting me down & doing so very rapidly. There are times when I put in some long hours here, but, I do not mind that because at the end of the month you have something to show for it & so have I. Not only that, but some of those people that used to come in to the shop with the whine, I have not had my Mirror, I have not had my Herald, or some other complaint used to get me down & I am afraid that if I had, had to stay there, this winter would have just about cooked my goose. I was feeling myself slipping from day to day.

Note the titles of the newspapers, both supporting Labour - which must have added to the offence when readers complained about the late delivery of their papers. No wonder Jim was glad when his son-in-law's brother – my Uncle Davy, big shot at Shell – found a ship for a final voyage to replenish the family finances. Meanwhile Norah searched for a buyer for the wretched shop and kept house for Ivor and his recently-acquired wife Greta living in the flat above it.

Jim's last ship was the MV *Port Said*, a cargo freighter owned by Shell's shipping company Anglo-Saxon, bound for Glasgow from Montreal. Times had been hard for more than twenty years, since the onset of the Depression. Jim was crossing the Atlantic just before the Coronation, which Norah and

Myf were due to attend, as they'd visited the Festival of Britain in 1951. His ship was overhauled by a liner full of Canadians on their way to the old country for the Coronation.

> There will be lots of money spent in London next week & it will certainly do a lot of good to all the hotels & shops. We can do with it & a spell of prosperity will do our country a lot of good, it's time it had some. What with one thing & the other it's had a pretty lean time of it for quite a number of years. A change will do a lot of good.

The last time Jim and Norah had known peace and prosperity and security would have been in the late 1920s, almost quarter of a century earlier. Decades of depression, war and austerity shaped my parents' outlook on life.

Jim's letters home from this last voyage display an outlook acquired during half a century at sea in the last decades of empire. Here's an extract from a letter written as he voyaged east through the Mediterranean in June 1953.

> I am now nearing Alexandria & as the majority of the crew live around there, you can naturally imagine that they are all agog with the prospect of being home in a day or two. Now is the period of the long fast Ramadan & it ends on the 12th of the month & as the ship will be at Alexandria then, they are all very pleased. As far as I can gather for these days there is a lot of feasting and jollification. Not drinking as that is contrary to the Moslem religion. I cannot help but admire the manner in which they carry out the period of fasting. From Sunrise to Sunset the devout Moslem – and there are a few of them on board – will not even take a drink of water. So you can imagine that in hot weather this is very tough on any person.

The tone is patronising but not lacking in regard. By this time the Free Officers had ousted King Farouk. Gamal Abdul Nasser was negotiating the terms of Britain's withdrawal from the Suez Canal Zone which it had garrisoned since the 1880s. Three years later he would puncture Britain's pretensions as an independent great power.

Jim's ship picked up a cargo in Alexandria and a solitary passenger, an elderly Indian woman returning to Bombay (as it still was). Soon he was again, as he put it in the time-honoured phrase, "east of Suez". He docked at Port Sudan (still controlled by Britain) to pick up 4,000 bales of cotton: "I have an assortment of cargo. Cotton for Bombay, Onions & Garlic for Colombo & Gypsum for Port Swettenham [in Malaya]." Here was a pattern of trade that Conrad would have recognised. Unlike Conrad, however, Jim was able to enjoy a morning swim in a sea-water pool as he voyaged south through the Red Sea.

After docking at Bombay the ship headed for the great port still called Calcutta, which Jim describes as "typically eastern".

> It is very remarkable that time does not mean a thing. I have watched some in this place just squat on their haunches & stay put the passage of time is unheeded. They seem to think that there is plenty of it and it is free. They say it takes all sorts of people to make a world & I must say I have met a fair share of all sorts of people. There is something about this India that I do not like, in fact I have never liked it. China is so different, that is a country that I would have stayed in had I gone there, if I had gone there when I was young. I do not remember anyone ever telling me that they did not like China. There is of course something very alluring about India & at the same time it's repellent. Lots of brilliant colouring in flowers & plants, but the flowers have not sweet smells, like ours. So where are we, what's the use of flowers without smell?

Jim exposes the prejudices of his generation in these remarks. John Darwin has described the "appalling" living conditions in Bombay which was noted in 1925 as possessing "the inglorious distinction of having probably the highest infant death rate in the world". In Calcutta the majority of people inhabited "unimaginably squalid and dangerous" shacks with no sanitation, while thousands slept in the streets. Three million people had died in surrounding Bengal in the famine of 1943. By contrast the great Chinese ports such as Shanghai, Canton and Hong Kong, which Jim would have visited in the last years of Western power, offered facilities matching those in great western cities even while the overwhelming majority of Chinese lived in greater poverty and squalor than in India. Jim filled his home with mementos from his voyages. I have in my bedroom the faded and worn but still lovely carpet – pink with a flamboyant blue and green flower pattern – that he brought home from China. Once it lay in the front room of Jim and Norah's last home in a gloomy Victorian terrace in South Shields, looking towards the Tyne from the back bedroom windows.

From Calcutta the ship turned west across the Indian Ocean and up the Red Sea and into the Mediterranean. By October it was navigating the Dardanelles on route for Constanza in Romania. In another letter Jim describes Gallipoli and recalls voyages before the First World War when Russia was a leading exporter of grain.

> I cannot see very much change, the monument is still standing at the entrance [to the Dardanelles] & the soldier's cemetery looks to be very well kept as usual. Being dark I could not see much of Istanbul & the Bosphorus. I cannot think that there will be any great changes there though. What a change around these parts as far as shipping is concerned, in my young days dozens of ships used to pass through these waters to & from the Black Sea, but today very few. The old Black Sea trade is dead & gone, it's a great pity as I loved the trade, within a few days one could tell when he would be back in England.

This last extract describes Constanza under Communist rule just after the death of Stalin.

> No doubt whatsoever about being on the wrong side of the Iron Curtain once in Roumania [sic]. This is really much worse than Russia, even there I have not experienced a soldier accompanying a Pilot when he boards a ship & follows him like a dog wherever he goes…. If this is their idea of The People's Republic, all I can say is that I am very glad indeed to think there is still a Britain in the world… Just fancy a ship lying at anchor in one of our own large ports, an armed guard stationed at the foot of the gangway with a list of the names of the various members of the crew, that were allowed ashore on any particular night. That is the position here. It's a great pity that some of the Comrades at home do not make a trip to Roumania as members of a ship's crew. I would be very interested to see their reaction… Of course Roumania is absolutely under the heel of Moscow & all the Public Works and Administrative Authority is under Russian control, so to all intents & purposes there is no Roumania any more. I have been to town on two occasions & all I could see was pictures

of Lenin & Stalin & lovely large signs in all languages Peace & Friendship. What a travesty of the words. When one walks along the street, what does one see, nothing but people in uniform men & women.

Jim, like my other grandfather, had been a Lloyd George Liberal, though by 1953 the great man's son Gwilym was serving as Minister of Food in Winston Churchill's government. This last voyage ended in Venice where Jim took the ship into dry dock. Then he'd have been on his way home to pick up the pieces after selling the newsagents' shop. Soon the family – he and Norah plus Ivor and Greta – would be off to South Shields and that gloomy terraced house in Mortimer Road.

Four years later, in March 1958, Jim died in hospital after falling from a bedroom window into the back yard. He might have suffered a dizzy spell while leaning out to clean the window, or he might have been gasping for air after suffering a heart attack or stroke. My father liked Jim – in a letter in 1976 he recalled his "irresistible smile" – though he never got on with Norah (for reasons I'll discuss in Chapter 4). He used say that Jim jumped to escape from her. That's when I heard about a second family in Australia – though not Norah's suicide attempt. Later my father would enlist me in his guerrilla operations against his surviving in-laws. Stock jokes about mothers-in-law held no surprise. I didn't like the gloomy house in Mortimer Road. I felt Jim become impatient with me as I grew. I was unmoved by his death. I didn't attend the funeral and my mother couldn't attend; she was confined to a hospital bed after an operation on her spine. Jim was buried in Harton Cemetery in the family plot purchased by Norah's father. She would have bought the headstone and chosen the inscription: "In Memory of My Beloved Husband... A Gallant Gentleman."

Norah lived on in Mortimer Road for 19 years, moving into a care home by the sea in Roker, Sunderland in 1977 after a spell with Ivor and his second wife Anne. Her home was dismantled and most of Jim's mementos were lost – apart from the carpet salvaged by Myf and a few pictures, plus a vicious Yemeni dagger that my mother passed to me. Norah died in January 1978.

Her ashes were interred with Jim's. Judging from her love of Longfellow I suspect she must have bought the edition of 'Hiawatha' that I loved as a boy. I might never have persisted as a diarist if she hadn't given me a first Five-Year Diary for Christmas in 1964 – and a second for Christmas in 1970. In 1976 she helped to pay for a holiday in Rhodes. I still have her last book token inscribed in a shaky hand "Wishing You A Happy Birthday & A Prosperous Future", from "Gran, With Love", which I've used as a bookmark. For years she would join the family for Christmas – for the last time in 1976. I would have seen her in 1977 if my parents had not chosen to spend Christmas in the Canary Islands. Weeks later she was dead. I returned to Sunderland for the funeral: "[t]he Minister gabled [sic] the service. I got to like Gran in her last years but I was never as close as Vanessa." Her granddaughter wasn't able to attend because she hadn't been told about it. Our mother didn't want to meet Vanessa because of what she regarded as an irregular romantic attachment.

Myf must have made the journey from Birmingham where she'd made a life. She worked as a saleswoman for IBM and then in the Mayoral office. She treasured a letter from Margaret Thatcher to her MP Jill Knight acknowledging her support during the miners' strike. Auntie Myf was a frequent visitor when I was a boy. She encouraged my interest in history. She'd never patronise, neither me nor Vanessa nor our sons. We'd discuss the Wars of the Roses, the first topic on which I acquired expert knowledge. I recall one of her boyfriends – Tommy, a gaunt man who'd spent years in a German prisoner of war camp. I met another, Arthur, when we visited Birmingham on the way home from holiday in 1965. Vanessa found photographs of them among Myf's papers after her death. In the 1970s she joined my mother on a sight-seeing holiday to Athens and then another to Florence where they fell out. She did much to fill the gap in the lives of my sons resulting from the premature loss of their maternal grandmother to Alzheimer's and my mother to cancer. Myf celebrated her 80th and 90th birthdays surrounded by friends and family, living in her own home until obliged by a falls to enter a care home. She'd already lost her mobility. Soon a series of strokes removed her capacity to speak coherently – but none of her indomitable spirit. She took pride in voting for Brexit. Covid killed her in February 2021 at the age of 96, just weeks after being vaccinated.

Ivor and Anne must have attended Norah's funeral in 1978. Greta appears in a family photograph taken on the beach at South Shields in the mid 1950s, but I believe she'd found another man by the end of the decade. Ivor continued to live with his widowed mother, moving in and out of unskilled jobs, including a spell as a warehouseman. In 1970 he met Anne at a working-man's club. They married in 1971. Big sister Mary drew a characteristically waspish and patronising portrait.

> Ivor's wedding went off quite well – she is like him, as deep as the ocean – one cannot tell what she is thinking. She is a big fat girl – utterly devoid of any kind of charm or poise, but her family are good steady people, with a very nice well-kept home & garden.

They had one daughter Shirley, born in 1971 and named for Ivor's twin. One day he walked out of this second marriage. He suffered more than one mental breakdown and spent time on the streets. My mother received a short letter around Christmas 1992. By then she was dying from cancer. She wrote a reply in a shaky hand and made out a cheque for £25 but was too ill to post the letter. Ivor drifted out of contact with Shirley who was discouraged by her grandmother from meeting him. She told me when I visited South Shields in September 2021 that he died un-mourned in a local authority care home in 2019, aged 89. The council paid for his funeral. Shirley found out about his death only because he'd left a small legacy and the council employed a solicitor to track her down as his closest kin.

Shirley lives in South Hylton by the Wear with her husband Lee and their Pug dog. They have no children. Lee works for Nissan and Shirley at a local Job Centre. Like Grandpa Jim, they support Sunderland. My mother, her aunt, took Shirley as a girl to visit her grandparents' grave in Harton Cemetery. She retained a dim memory of the location of the plot and the inscription to the infant who'd borne her name. Shirley decided that the right place to inter Myf's ashes was in this family plot. She and Lee found it and cleaned and tidied it up. They filled an urn with most of the ashes and cemented it in place at the centre of the plot. The remaining ashes they consigned to the North Sea.

Chapter 3

Captain Jim's Wrist Watch

During a lifetime at sea, Capt James Williams...came face to face with death on many occasions. He survived shipwreck and was rescued from the Atlantic after his ship was torpedoed and sunk. Countless times he overcame misfortune on the high seas.

(*Shields Gazette*, 18 March 1958)

As he sat in his study in Ballylee Tower near Galway in the 1920s W B Yeats (he preferred to be known by his initials, like D H Lawrence) would find inspiration in a 550-year old samurai sword wrapped in fragile silk given by a young Japanese admirer Junzo Sato: "Two heavy trestles, and a board / Where Sato's gift, a changeless sword, / By pen and paper lies,... / A bit of an embroidered dress / Covers its wooden sheath" ('Meditations in Time of Civil War': III *My Table*). Instead of contemplating a sword of hammered steel I can open a blue velvet case to view my grandfather's wrist watch.

My mother described herself in a letter in 1969 as "still an old Romantic at heart!" As a girl she'd loved the novels of Alexandre Dumas. I recall well-thumbed blue soft-covered editions of *The Three Musketeers, Twenty Years After, Louise de La Valliere* and *The Vicomte de Bragelonne* on our shelves. If she'd been a 17th century Gascon nobleman like old Monsieur d'Artagnan, she might have given her son a sword as he set out to win his fortune. Instead, she gave me her father's wrist watch one day when I was 14 or 15, after I'd broken my small round Timex. I wore this watch every day until I was almost 50 when I inherited my father's.

The watch is nothing special: a gold-plated Tissot *antimagnetique*, an innovative design in its day and manufactured in thousands in many variants in the 1930s and 1940s. My mother told me that her father had bought it in the late 1930s. Now it would look like a woman's watch. Then it was called a dress watch, slim and rectangular and little more than an inch long and about three-quarters of an inch wide. The sides have a light Art Deco curve. The face is stained and spotted. In the 1990s I had to have it repaired and re-plated after friction from my wrist wore a hole in the back and stopped the mechanism. Soon after having it repaired I started wearing my father's watch. Now Captain Jim's watch lies in its blue case, with a new strap and fresh gold-plating, with only the foxed face to betray its age.

My mother told me little about her father apart from the facts that he'd been a merchant navy captain who'd served through both world wars and had been torpedoed in the second. The papers I inherited from his womenfolk leave no doubt about their admiration. Twenty years ago Myf insisted I should take good care of a bundle of his papers that she handed to me. In conversation she'd give full voice to her pride and love. I'm glad she had a chance to read an early version of this chapter before she died.

After Gran's funeral I took the train back to London and visited a girlfriend who lived round the corner from my flat in Hampstead. A previous boyfriend had taught her to restore paintings and furniture and now she did a bit of modelling and dealt in art in a small way. From her I discovered how having a man of action as a father can form a woman. As she told his story, he'd been an officer of Gurkhas in the Second World War and then during the anti-Communist "Emergency" in Malaya in the late 1940s. He'd gone on to serve in the SAS and had fought against Communist insurgents in Oman in the 1960s. He was a fighting soldier and chose to enter Civvy Street rather than steer a desk. After failing in his own small business he'd become a manager in a car hire company by the late 1970s. One evening in 1979 he treated us to dinner in his club in Newcastle under Lyme and then took us home to drink whisky. My friend was his only daughter, but he passed on more of his spirit to her than to any of his sons, one with "learning difficulties" and a passion for Cliff Richard, another a policeman and then a private soldier in Northern Ireland, and the third a roustabout on oil rigs in the North Sea.

When we parted after four years I was left feeling that no man could ever match her father. Her mother wanted her to marry, but my friend seemed to hold her in little regard and to prefer *la vie boheme* over life as the wife of a Whitehall official. My mother, equally formidable in her own way, was determined to marry. She chose a gentle, handsome man who was unable to match the high expectations she'd derived from her father. As compensation she invested her disappointed hopes in me. She gave me her father's watch.

All three of Jim's womenfolk took newspaper cuttings of his maritime exploits. The unvarnished prose on fragile yellowing paper conveys those events more vividly than paraphrase or elaboration. Two of his exploits involved rescues from foundering sailing ships in the North Atlantic. John Darwin has described it as "perhaps the most hazardous of all major seas" with ice and fog and tempestuous winter storms.

The first rescue was in February 1923 about 30 miles west of Cape Finisterre, when Jim was chief officer of the steamer *Jerseymoor*.

> At the time there was a very heavy gale blowing from the W.S.W. which subsequently shifted to the N.W. This fact caused the already high sea to take on a very confused character and became correspondingly more dangerous.
>
> Such were the conditions when the schooner Delfina was sighted flying signals of distress. Despite the danger involved progress was immediately made towards the stricken vessel, when it was ascertained that she was leaking badly and the crew desired to be taken off with all haste.
>
> Steering to windward of the sailing vessel, oil was lavishly distributed from the Jerseymoor with a view to smoothing out the sea, so far as was possible, in order to render the work of rescue less hazardous.
>
> The lifeboat was then launched from the steamer under the command of the chief officer, assisted by the second officer, and manned by a volunteer crew of four able seamen.
>
> Drifting down with the wind and protected by the film of oil over the water, the schooner was quickly reached and her entire crew safely embarked. Then the most dangerous portion of the journey had to be undertaken, as the boat had to be manoeuvred over sea unimpeded by oil, down to leeward, in order to make once more the steamer, which had been moved

to the leeside of the schooner; it being of course, impossible to pull to windward in the teeth of the gale.

In this manner, by the exercise of good seamanship, the whole of the crew of the schooner were [sic] safely transferred to the Jerseymoor, though the weather was such that the lifeboat was smashed and had to be abandoned.

One might ask: how on earth did they manage to scramble to safety while Jim controlled the lifeboat as it was being smashed to pieces against the side of the ship? He and his shipmates were awarded medals and diplomas for gallantry by the Portuguese Consul in a ceremony in Swansea attended by representatives of the Board of Trade, the Maritime Board, the Imperial Merchant Service Guild and the owners of the *Jerseymoor*.

The second featured on the front and back pages of the *North Mail* and *Newcastle Daily Chronicle* for 15 March 1926. This time Jim was second in command of the liner *Vinemoor*, when one evening in mid Atlantic they encountered another sailing ship, the *Novelty*, firing off distress signals. The *Vinemoor* approached and Captain Thomas Sisterson hailed the *Novelty* through a megaphone. The captain of the schooner asked to be rescued with his crew of seven.

As Sisterson, a real old salty dog judging from the photograph on the back page of the paper, told its reporter

They had no boat… and the rudder and sails were gone. I said I would send my lifeboat out to them, and at once asked for volunteers from my crew. I had no trouble in this respect…. I must say, however, that I was very pleased that my apprentices were as keen as any to have a hand in work that, in view of the heavy sea and in darkness, was not without danger.

Note the studied under-statement. Chief officer Jim took the tiller of the lifeboat, helped by the third officer, two seamen and a couple of apprentices. Sisterson continued

There was a heavy sea running and the darkness added to the difficulty of the task of rescue. As the schooner was absolutely out of control, I had to lie about a mile away from her.

The lifeboat had great difficulty in coming alongside the vessel, as she was rolling very heavily, but at last the crew were taken off and brought aboard my vessel, and were very naturally in an exhausted condition.

The captain told me that he had been out 22 days from Newfoundland, for the Brazils, with a cargo of salt fish. He had experienced bad weather all the time having lost the rudder after two days, and afterwards the sails.

The schooner had become ice bound, so intense was the cold, and as they were unable to pump the vessel they had jettisoned about 90 tons of cargo to lighten her.

Before leaving the schooner the crew set it on fire to eliminate a threat to other ships, so Sisterson had to steer well clear of the blazing derelict ship.

I had manoeuvred [my] ship to make a lee side for the rescue boat, and after getting the men on board I tried to pick the boat up, but found I could not do so without great danger of loss of life. She had been badly damaged, and I decided to abandon her.

This was the second time Jim had to abandon the lifeboat following a rescue. He'd have had to pass the exhausted rescued crew up the side of his ship and to control the lifeboat until all his shipmates had scrambled on board. Only then would he have followed them. The article concludes

None of the rescuing crew had much to say about their experience, except to express their pleasure at having been able to be of service to fellow sailors. 'It might have been us who wanted saving,' quietly observed one.

On the back page there's a fine portrait of Captain Sisterson, wearing his cap and pea-jacket, with a fag in one hand and the other in his trouser pocket, and the charming photograph of the rescuers, with Jim holding the ship's cat, which I've placed at the head of this chapter.

On 28 June 1927 the *Shields Daily Gazette and Shipping Telegraph* devoted a column to a report of a presentation on behalf of the Government of Newfoundland at a special meeting of the Newcastle Local Marine Board. Jim was awarded a sextant, third officer F G Nesbit a pair of binoculars, with

£12 to be shared by the other four men. His wife and daughter Mary (aged 10) would have attended.

The Lord Mayor gave a sketch of "the dramatic happenings of that dark February night in the Atlantic, in the midst of mountainous seas. It took cool courage of the enduring sort to go out in a frail lifeboat under such conditions to assist those in peril." Characteristically he called them "true British heroes". Equally characteristically Jim and Nesbit said simply that they were "glad to receive the gifts which had been given to them for what they considered to be a very simple act of duty." Jim had earned the command of a ship on his next voyage.

Young Jim was unscathed by the First World War but his luck ran out in the second when, as he entered his sixth decade, he assumed command of the *Kingston Hill* in May 1941. Judging from a passing reference in one of his letters from 1953 Jim might have been offered the ship while he was working as a pilot on the Clyde. It was a sleek modern tramp steamer, built on the Clyde only a year previously, but it turned out to be an unlucky ship.

When Jim took command in an emergency the ship was carrying a load of coal for Cape Town and Alexandria. Here's the story, told by an anonymous survivor of the ship's single, fatal voyage, from an undated cutting.

> We were 600 miles from Ireland, south of Iceland, when a four-engined Focke-Wulf bombed us while in convoy. They got a near miss which flooded our engine-room. Nobody was injured, but our captain...died from shock that night. Tugs came out and towed us 700 miles back to Scotland. We spent some months being repaired.
>
> We set out again for Cape Town in May, with a new captain [Jim]. We were torpedoed on June 7 in mid Atlantic [south west of Cape Verde, about half way between West Africa and Brazil]. The torpedo struck us without warning in No. 4 hold just after nine o'clock in the evening. The engine-room caught fire and soon the whole midship section was ablaze.
>
> Most of the engine-room crew escaped to the deck, but owing to the flames, it was impossible to stop the engines. The ship took a list to starboard and we thought she was going to turn over.

About 200 feet of the ship's side was blown in by the torpedo. The starboard lifeboats and the starboard side of the bridge [where Jim probably would have been standing] were blown away. The remaining two lifeboats were lowered as quickly as possible, though the ship was still travelling at practically full speed.

The first lifeboat could not be unhooked from the falls in time, and up-ended as soon as it touched the water. Its crew were thrown out, and eight men were drowned.

Meanwhile the fourth engineer, Mr. W. Matthew, was trapped in the shaft tunnel, where he had been examining the bearings when the torpedo hit. Immediately after the explosion the tunnel had been closed by one of engineers, who was not aware that the fourth engineer was inside.

The second engineer, Mr. J. Toms, when he learned that Mr. Matthews was trapped in the tunnel, made a gallant attempt to re-enter the engine-room to release him, and also to shut off the engines. The engine-room was an inferno, however, and he was driven back by the flames.

Eventually Mr. Matthew turned up in the crew's quarters in the poop [the stern], having managed to get out of the tunnel through an escape hatch.

After about ten minutes the ship stopped of her own accord, and some of us got away in the remaining boat. Some took to rafts and others jumped into the sea. The captain was among those who escaped on a raft.

Jim would have been the last to leave the ship. Apart from the eight men drowned when the first lifeboat was lost, another six men were thrown into the hold when the hatch on which they were sitting collapsed as the torpedo struck. Only two of them, a Chinese sailor and a gunner, were saved.

Meanwhile, as the ship was slowly foundering, the U-boat appeared out of the night.

While we were taking to the boats the submarine surfaced and cruised about at some distance, showing a light occasionally. The ship sank after about half-an-hour. We rowed about and picked up the captain and other men from the rafts and four who were swimming. After the ship had sunk the submarine went off without trying to find out what ship she had sunk.

She passed close to us, but did not try to communicate. We heard her Diesels distinctly. The light she was showing played on the conning tower and we saw her number – U-37.

This is one of the most interesting parts of the story. The *Kingston Hill* was sailing alone and not in convoy. The U-boat would have over-hauled the ship during the day and then lain in wait until night fell when it would have approached on the surface before firing a single torpedo right amidships.

The narrator was obviously puzzled about why the U-boat approached and cruised around showing its lights while the survivors struggled to save themselves. The commander was taking a risk: he'd have been a sitting duck in the (albeit unlikely) event that an aircraft or a warship had happened on the scene. Almost certainly he was making sure that all of the survivors had been hauled from the sea before disappearing back into the night.

I'm reminded of a famous episode in September 1942 in the same part of Atlantic when U-156 commanded by Korvetten-Kapitan Werner Hartenstein surfaced after torpedoing the liner RMS *Laconia* carrying 3,000 passengers. Hartenstein collected several lifeboats containing about 200 survivors and radioed for help from German and Italian U-boats and Vichy French warships based in Dakar. Eventually two other U-boats came to help and the three of them were shepherding several lifeboats towards safety when the little convoy was attacked by a long-range US Air Force Liberator bomber and the U-boats forced to dive to save themselves. Grand-Admiral Karl Doenitz, commander of U-boats, would be indicted at Nuremburg for his subsequent order forbidding U-boats to attempt similar rescues in future. U-156 was sunk with all hands a few months later.

The U-boat that attacked Jim's ship couldn't have been U-37 because it had already completed its final patrol in March 1941, before being withdrawn for training. In fact the *Kingston Hill* seems to have been sunk by U-38 commanded by Kapitan-Leutnant Heinrich Liebe, aged 33 at the time. Liebe was the fourth highest-scoring U-boat commander in the Second World War, responsible for sinking almost 190,000 tons of Allied shipping. This would be his last patrol. On returning to Germany he'd travel to the Wolf's Lair in East Prussia to receive the Knight's Cross with oak leaves, Nazi Germany's highest military honour, from the hands of Adolf Hitler.

He'd spend the rest of the war on Doenitz's staff planning U-boat operations and would go home to Eisenach in the Soviet occupation zone after the war. He refused to serve in the East German Navy. He never married and spent the rest of his life in various menial jobs. He died aged 89 in 1997, surviving Jim by almost 40 years. Rarely in modern war can we identify the leading protagonists. Liebe's U-boat also survived the war, to be scuttled in the Weser estuary in May 1945.

Now the survivors were alone in the South Atlantic hundreds of miles from land.

> The 32 of us were left alone in our two lifeboats, one of which was damaged and had lost its mast, sail and oars when it capsized. We found the wreckage of one of the other lifeboats and managed to salve a tin of biscuits from it. At dawn we started off for the South American coast, which we estimated was about 800 miles away.
>
> Between the two boats we had only eight oars and one mast and sail, and this handicapped us greatly, but we improvised a sail for one boat out of the boat cover. We rationed each man to half a biscuit and half a gill [one eighth of a pint] of water twice a day.
>
> So we sailed, or more correctly drifted, day after day. We had no water troubles, fortunately, for it rained several times during the early part of the voyage. We only had thin clothes, however, and one of the men had no clothes at all during the 13 days in the boats.
>
> When we were not drenched with water, we were blistered by the terrible heat of the sun. Most of us broke out in blisters and boils.
>
> On the tenth day we saw a ship, but it was sailing away. They did not see us. We were then running short of water. That night the captain brought the two boats together and told us all frankly that we were in a desperate plight. He suggested that we should all pray for water. We did so. The very next day we got all the rain we could collect.
>
> On the following evening the captain again called us together and suggested that we should pray for a ship to pick us up. He prayed that if possible it should be an American ship [a nice touch: presumably the grub would be better than on a British ship].
>
> We were none of us religious, but we all knew that the way those prayers were answered was not just a coincidence. At two o'clock the next morning

a rain squall cleared and the second officer saw a ship coming along. We fired a flare and we learned afterwards that the people on the ship thought it was a submarine and wanted to run for it, but they found they were too near.

Then we flashed by morse lamp: 'British survivors: could you pick us up?' The ship flashed back: 'O.K.'

It was an American freighter [The Alabaman] on her way to Cape Town. Those Americans treated us swell. They could not have treated us better. So we reached Cape Town after all, having taken six months for the voyage and lost our ship and some of our mates on the way.

Jim was 50. He wasn't the oldest. 64-year old Joe Lawson had been torpedoed in the First World War and planned to leave the sea at the end of this voyage. "Despite his age he was pulling an oar with the rest of his shipmates after 12 days in the lifeboat." Another survivor had already been torpedoed three times in as many years: "'I'm going back to sea again right away" he said today. 'I've been torpedoed in 1939, 1940 and 1941, so I shouldn't be due for another one for six months at least!" Another had been torpedoed in October 1940 and picked up by a destroyer after four hours in a boat.

Looking back they seem like another breed of men. Now this kind of stoical courage seems inconceivable, but for Jim and his crew it seems to have been literally all in a day's work. The Second World War demanded all kinds of courage: the courage to face the risk of incineration in a brewed-up tank; the courage to charge into exploding shrapnel or machine-gun fire; the courage to sit for hours in a bomber's rear gun-turret keeping your eyes peeled for a German night-fighter; or the courage to take split-second decisions in a dog fight over the English Channel. A special kind of courage was needed to endure the risk of a sudden torpedo at any moment; and then, after your ship had gone down and you'd scrambled into an open lifeboat, to hold the survivors together for almost two weeks in the middle of the Atlantic. Fortunately Jim and his shipmates were near the Equator or they would never have survived.

As well as the fading newsprint from which I've been quoting so liberally, I inherited the letter that Jim sent to Norah while he was recovering in a comfortable hotel in Cape Town. It's dated 20 July and Norah has noted that it arrived on 27 August. It's the only one of his letters to have survived apart from a dozen or so from the late 1940s and early 1950s from which I've quoted in Chapter 2. Norah and her children would have been informed in June that Jim's ship had been lost. They'd have spent weeks without knowing whether he was alive or dead.

Jim begins by saying that he doesn't know when the letter will reach Norah. He goes on

> Taking all things into account we are not doing so badly. I am really very pleased to know that Germany is getting well & truly pasted by the R.A.F. & I hope they will keep on with the good work. I had very little love for the Germans before, but now I have nothing but a very bitter loathing for them, which will always continue when the war is over. They are really worse than swine, in fact it's an insult to the swine to couple them with the Nazis.
>
> I am very pleased to be able to tell you that I am getting over our experience. It was tough while it lasted, but the good food & treatment which we received on the 'Alabaman' and the rest here has certainly made a wonderful difference.

By this time the other survivors were on their way home. Perhaps Jim spent longer in Cape Town because of injury. His feet suffered lasting damage from immersion in sea water in the bilge of the lifeboat. He might have lost toes from the equivalent of trench foot. Already he'd been asked to take over another ship.

> I felt that it was my duty to do so. Had I turned it down, it's quite possible that they would bring pressure to bear & more or less compel me to go & that's the one thing I did not wish to happen & another thing we must do all we can to beat these damned Jerrys. It's a hard job, but I really & truly think he is getting a real hiding these days & he will get more as each day passes. I think that to all intents & purposes he is on the run now. Russia was not so easy a job for him. It appears he is in a bit of a mess

regarding Russia, especially the way they are burning everything & not leaving anything at all that can be used by the Germans. I must say that it's very apparent that next winter will be terribly hard in Russia. There will be no crops in Russia & hardly anything in the other countries, so it cannot be anything but a very hard & bitter times that faces them all.

How right he was. The crumbling syntax betrays the depth of feeling. This passage helps to explain the admiration felt by ordinary Britons for the sacrifices of the Soviet people against a vicious common enemy.

The letter ends by looking forward to peace: "What a treat it will be when it's all over & the world at large returns to sanity. It's almost too good to be true too when one thinks & looks forward to the return to normal conditions." Meanwhile he's enjoying the peace and fine weather in Cape Town: "A few more days of rest & quietness & I think I'll be ready for the road again". As indeed he would be.

I don't know how Jim spent the rest of the war. Perhaps he took command of another ship. Perhaps he went back to work as a pilot. All I know is that he would never face the same kind of ordeal as in 1941. I'll close the case containing his wrist watch and return it to the drawer in my study where it will rest until one of my sons straps it on to his wrist and the other fastens my father's watch.

Chapter 4
Portrait of a Marriage

I am not by nature a domesticated woman, & I preferred to be out in the world once caring for my home & my family was no longer a full time job.

(Mary Williams, to the author, 8 February 1969)

You must realize now that what you do and say is extremely important to Mam, and in the past you have been too free with her. I have to act the same way with her – she is not to be trifled with, so I hope you'll be a wise fella in your future relations. I don't know what she has said to you but don't treat it lightly: she can be terribly hard if she thinks it necessary – as she has been with me at times.

(John [Jack] Williams, to the author, 15 February 1969)

I've chosen these passages, from letters found while clearing the garage after completing the first draft of this memoir, as emblematic of the contrasting personalities of my parents – and of relations between them.

My parents would have been planning their wedding during the summer of 1941, while Mary worried about her father lost at sea. By the time of the wedding in October in Streatham, where she'd lived during the winter of the Blitz, she would have known he was safe, though not yet back in Britain. Jack's father had only weeks to live (until November) and would have been in no condition to make the trip, while his mother would have had to remain in South Shields to nurse her dying husband. The only family members to attend the wedding were Mary's mother Norah and her sister Myfanwy.

I've placed the smaller of two group photographs of the wedding at the head of this chapter but even the larger one shows only twelve people apart from bride and groom. A newspaper cutting made by Norah describes her daughter as wearing "an ensemble of French wool blue georgette and a picture hat, with a burgundy-tinted veil to match. A spray of blue orchids was fastened to her jacket, and she carried an ivory-bound Prayer Book."

Myfanwy, just turned 17, wore "a dress of dusty-pink crepe marocain and a navy blue hat" and held a bouquet of anemones. Jack wore his RAF uniform. This was an austere wartime wedding, like my mother's parents must have been in 1916 – and my son David's was in October 2020, as Covid gathered force in its second wave.

I've told how one pair of grandparents, on my father's side, was late Victorian. The other, on my mother's side, belonged to the Generation of 1914. My parents belonged to what Americans have described, with characteristic sentimental exaggeration, as "the Greatest Generation" – the one born during the second decade of the century. I prefer to call it the generation of the Depression, which began in 1930 and shaped their youth. As young adults this generation fought the Second World War and afterwards, as they formed families, endured a decade of austerity. In middle age they enjoyed growing affluence from the late 1950s until the economy shuddered to a halt in the mid 1970s. As they approached old age, some would support Margaret Thatcher's bid to restore the stability they'd known in their prime. Others would endure the transformation of established industrial communities and the loss of livelihoods they'd expected to pass to their children.

For children, the most mysterious parts of their parents' lives happened before they met. I've inherited few written records of these years but several albums with photographs from this period, from which I've tried to reconstruct their lives before they met in South Shields in 1938. I'll use these albums to explicate, so far as I can, a mystery in the youth of each of them, and I'll try to explain how such contrasting, perhaps ill-assorted, people – gentle soul and turbulent spirit – came together. I'll go on to describe the early years of their marriage and the difficulties they encountered during my childhood – difficulties that must have played a large part in shaping me. I'll canter over later years, beginning in my teens, when they played a diminishing part in my life, until their deaths in the 1990s.

I'll begin with my father, born in 1910, christened John but always called Jack. I've called him the Benjamin of the family, born when his father was 45 and his mother nearing 40. Jack grew up in a first-floor flat in a terrace on the southern edge of a rapidly growing port (home to 110,000 people by 1911) surrounded by siblings approaching adulthood. In his last letter his brother Davy, older by ten years, described Jack as "a wonderful and much-loved youngster." In a letter after my father's death his nephew David told me how his mother Peggie always regarded Jack as "her little brother". Jack would have been raised mainly by women: his mother and sisters Winnie and Peggie. His father doesn't seem to have been much of a presence. Young Jack would have walked to the sea-front less than a mile away. He'd have wandered along the cliffs to Marsden and out into the country around Cleadon. As a boy I loved to hear him talk about the First World War. He recalled soldiers on leave from France with mud on their uniforms. He saw a biplane land on the school playing field. He was taught by women and aging men; the young men had gone to war. He visited Bronco Bill's travelling circus and saw Red Indians and Cowboys. He laughed at the silent films of Charlie Chaplin.

Consult any substantial biography of Hitler or Stalin and you'll find the familiar sort of school photograph with the tyrant aged around 10 standing among his class-mates in the middle of the back row. Apparently young Djugashvili chose that spot. Perhaps young Schicklgruber did too. I've inherited two similar photographs showing my father around the same age: one from 1919 (when he'd have been 8 or 9) and the other from 1921 (aged 10 or 11). You can immediately spot the two tyrants; their faces leap from the photographs. I had to ask Vanessa to help in identifying my father. Then I saw him – a neatly dressed lad, with a kind open face, among rough and tough urchins.

Jack was never going to set the world on fire. During six years of war service in the RAF, he never rose above the rank of Leading Aircraftman (equivalent to Lance-Corporal). Each morning I strap on the wrist watch he was awarded in 1965 for 35 years of service in the North East Electricity Board. When as a lecturer I had occasion to discuss the vanished notion of 'the career for life' in classes on the Sociology of Work, I would unfasten the watch and recite the inscription on the back: "N.E.E.B " on the upper rim and "ELECTRICITY SUPPLY" on the lower, with "J WILLIAMS 1930 – 1965" at the centre. My punch line was that my father had another 10 years to serve. In 45 years (broken by six years of war service) he never rose above Senior Accounts Clerk. He spent decades preparing bills for customers and compiling records of payment, tasks already starting to be performed by computers by the time he retired in 1975. He never qualified as an accountant, though that was how his wife would describe him. He must have been thinking about his own working life when in a letter of 1969 he complained that "clerical working hours...are far too long. It is a real strain to keep your head down for eight hours a day, especially if the people you work for are what is known as 'pushers.'" My father was no pusher. He didn't intend a compliment when he described me as a born boss. He was full of encouragement when I resigned from the civil service in 1995, three years before he died, to start a second career as a university lecturer.

My father wrote in a letter in 1979: "I left school the day I was fourteen" – that is, 30 November 1924. Since 1918 14 had been the standard school-leaving age. As posterity we condescend too readily towards our forbears. I found on the first of the two class photographs, the one taken in 1919, the words "Westoe Road School" in pencil in my father's hand. The wall in the background looks grim enough. In reality Westoe Road School was one of tens of thousands of so-called Board Schools built by over 2,500 School Boards between their inception under the Elementary Education Act of 1870 and replacement under the Education Act of 1902 with 330 local education authorities. Westoe Road was one of the largest in the country, built in open country not far from my father's home and opened in 1890 with places for 2,000 pupils. Jack would have entered the Infants School, accommodating around 560 pupils, in 1914 or 1915. Three years later he'd have moved to the main building, two storeys high, with places for 500 boys on the first floor and an equal number of girls on the ground floor. Here he'd stay until 1924, progressing through seven standards of attainment not only in the 3 Rs (reading, writing and arithmetic) but also rules of grammar, composition, literature, history, geography, drawing, geometry, algebra and elementary science. He'd have been examined in each standard and taken home reports to his parents twice a year. He'd have left with a School Leaving Certificate recording the standard he'd achieved and the headmaster's comments on his character and conduct. Few if any elementary schools would have offered a better education.

Jack's mother would have felt protective towards her youngest child. Her firstborn Winnie had died in 1923. Her second son Sam must have been sickening with the tuberculosis that would kill him in 1925. They remained a presence for their brother. He ensured that his children knew about their lost aunt and uncle. Jack's mother wouldn't have wanted him to go to sea like her husband and oldest son Davy. His parents would have needed him to bring money into the home now that his father, nearing 60, must have had difficulty finding work. Then men had to wait until they were 70 before they could draw a pension. For the next 15 years Jack and his surviving sister Peggie would be the main earners. No wonder my father was frugal to the point of meanness.

His first job was in a billiard hall, stacking balls and serving drinks. Then he worked for a firm of maritime stores dealers – Joures & Maltman in South Shields. I have a studio photograph taken on his 16th birthday in 1926, while he was working there. It shows a smart young man, wearing a double-breasted suit, hair pomaded and neatly parted, with an open face and a light smile. He was probably being paid as an apprentice likely to be dismissed when he reached 18 and his employers became liable for National Insurance contributions. Here's what happened to a young man apprenticed to a butcher for 5/- (25p) a week rising to 7/6 (about 40p).

When I got to about eighteen I came to ten shillings [50p] a week and he [the butcher] couldn't pay me any more. He said 'I'll give you a reference, and that's about all I can do for you. I just hope you can get a job.' So that's when I had my first experience of the dole.

This young man would have qualified for a non-contributory benefit ("the dole") because he wouldn't have paid any National Insurance – though he'd need to show that he was looking for employment. Something similar must have happened to Jack. He was dismissed with a letter dated July 1928 addressed 'To Whom It May Concern' stating that he had been employed as "Apprentice Sales in the Furniture Department for the last two and a half years. He has always behaved himself well and has given us satisfaction in his work. We found him to be honest, reliable, and obliging in his manner. He leaves us owing to staff reduction and through no fault of his own and takes with him our best wishes for his future career." Jack was some months short of 18, without obvious prospects.

He did have one huge asset: for all the shy manner and modest ability, Jack was growing into an exceptionally good-looking young man, tall and handsome with a fine physique. I can say so with confidence because after his death I found an album containing what can fairly be described as homo-erotic photographs taken on holiday in the Lake District with two other men in 1932 when he was aged 21. This was a special presentation album from the oldest of the three men. A second, ordinary album contains lots of similar photographs.

My father never mentioned either of these albums, though he did tell me about an older man who had taken him under his wing, so to speak, after he left the maritime stores dealers. This was probably the Norman who inscribed "with warmest wishes for his majority" in 1931 a slim volume of *Twenty Poems from Rudyard Kipling* with the ribbon marking 'If – '. My father told me that this man encouraged him to study for the qualifications that enabled him to secure a position in South Shields Borough Council in 1930 (the date on his watch). Then local councils were responsible for electricity supply, before the industry was nationalised by the Labour Government after the Second World War. Jack worked in the department responsible for billing customers. His mentor also encouraged him to take part in amateur dramatics and to develop an interest in light opera and musical comedy. My mother listed amateur operatics among his interests, with golf, cricket, rugby and walking, in the album she compiled in the 1980s. I've inherited a good number of photographs, extending well into middle age, showing him in theatrical costume – including one as a fetching Joseph from 1932, the year of his holiday in the Lake District. My shelves contain my father's copy of R C Sherriff's *Journey's End* published in 1929. By family tradition he took the part of the young officer, straight from school, in an amateur production.

The presentation album contains only 18 photographs but they're all skilfully shot and carefully mounted with slightly arch comments. The title page sets the tone, with the words (on flimsy paper overlying a pair of photographs on sturdier paper): "THESE SUPERB WORKS OF ART ARE DEDICATED TO JACK WILLIAMS (hereinafter referred to as the 'Black Villain'"). These two photographs show the cottage overlooking Ullswater where the three men must have stayed. Others show them outside Wordsworth's Cottage in Grasmere, or my father with the young man styled 'The Red Villain' and an older man, self-styled 'The Professor' (presumably the Norman who'd inscribed the Kipling volume). At the head of this chapter I've placed a photograph from the ordinary album showing these men on either side of my father. Most of the photographs in the presentation album show only my father. In one he's wearing a singlet and shorts and wielding the oars in a rowing boat. In a second he's sitting in swimming trunks on the gunwales of the boat, holding a towel behind his neck with one end in each hand. Two show him emerging from a lake in an old-fashioned swimming costume covering his torso. One shows only his head and shoulders; the other includes his torso. I wonder if 'The Professor' compiled a companion album for the less fetching 'Red Villain'?

The second album is one that my father must have begun to compile around the same time, as it contains more photographs from the same holiday, and others in which he appears around the same age – in his early 20s. This album contains about a hundred photographs. The subjects are mainly male. There's one of Jack among a group of young men and women, and two or three with older women, but none showing signs of intimacy. There are two shots of his elder brother Davy, one in full officer's rig. The rest are male. Lots show Jack in beach wear, including this exceptionally striking photograph, larger than the others and occupying its own page in the album.

Another photograph shows him with shirt open to the waist and an arm over the shoulder of a smaller man. In several he's wearing the same combination of shorts and body-hugging diamond-patterned Fair Isle sweater. There's no getting away from it: in these photographs we're looking at my father through queer eyes. Several show 'The Professor', who must have taken many of them. One shows a smart car in a rural setting, at a time when there were only about a million on the road in Britain. It must have belonged to 'The Professor', who'd have used it to drive the two young 'Villains' to the Lake District.

When I found these two albums I felt as though I was stepping into the world of Christopher Isherwood and Joe Ackerley. I recall talking to my father about these years. He mentioned an older man who must have been 'The Professor' and the Norman who inscribed the volume of Kipling. My father often talked about a memorable holiday in the Lake District, which he'd visit with my mother many times during the 1940s. So what was going on? 'The Professor' looks ten or fifteen years older than the young men. He might have been an officer in the war. He was obviously an educated man, a schoolmaster or a university lecturer. At a time when there were just over a million cars on the roads of Britain he had the means to run a smart saloon and to take two young men on holiday. Today we might assume that there was some kind of sexual relationship. I think we'd be mistaken.

Noel Annan is level-headed about relations between what he describes as "Hellenistic dons and schoolmasters" and working class youths: "it can be safely said about most of these bachelors that they were never guilty of any homosexual act that was criminal according to the law of the land." Each of the two 'Villains' would have acted as a chaperone to the other. Annan goes on

> These homosexuals often found sexual satisfaction only outside their own class. They admired virile, tough, working-class men – men who appeared to be normal heterosexuals – and very often were normal. Sometimes they would be younger men and their lovers took pleasure in giving them a good time, making them companions without spoiling them. Joe Ackerley found 'working class boys more unreserved, and understanding, friendship with them opened up interesting areas of life, hitherto unknown'.

From all I know of my father, I doubt whether he engaged in sexual relations with 'The Professor'. You only have to read E M Forster's tale of homosexual love *Maurice*, completed in 1914 but not published until 1971 following his death, to realise how wary such a man would have been about seeking "union" with a young working-class man. What probably happened was that an educated older man, almost certainly gay in today's terms, took a shine to a handsome, gentle young man whom he'd have met through chapel or a young men's club and taken under his wing. He would have encouraged Jack to obtain the qualification that enabled him to find a secure job. He could afford to treat young men to holidays where they could display their bodies. He might have enjoyed some manly embraces. In short, 'The Professor' was probably no more than a substitute for the attentive father Jack never knew.

As the 1930s wore on, this man seems to have faded from his life. My father was characteristically reticent about these years. I would prompt him about the turbulent politics of the time but he told me that he was absorbed in sport and amateur operatics. Only once did he enlarge on his inner life, in a letter sent in May 1973 during a difficult period in my own life. A lengthy relationship had come to a sudden and a bad end. I was struggling to complete a PhD thesis and applying unsuccessfully for a string of lecturing jobs just as Conservative public spending cuts began to bite. He told me

> I found my twenties the hardest years of my life and that's the truth. My late teens [when he met the Professor] were the best. I think living is bound up with some sort of pattern to do with discovery and staleness, and like you, I had some strong emotional struggles. Then it was not a permissive society and I suppose I was dominated by my imagination. When I used to fall for someone I broke off relations when I thought it got too serious, and then fretted about it. When I had to live through bad patches, I used to fall back on Kipling's 'If' and the line "And so hold on when there is nothing in you except the Will which says 'Hold on.'" Another thought was about Christiana in Pilgrim's Progress, when she was in the Slough of Despond, her simple solution was to take steps to get out of it. I always found great strength in religion. I maintain it is the greatest joy in the world. I have allowed it to be shuffled out of mind but the thought of bringing it back is always there.

During this period he was living with elderly parents in the first-floor flat in which he'd grown up with siblings who had either died or, like Davy, left home. After Peggie married in the mid 1930s he'd have been the only earner. His father wouldn't have qualified for the state pension until 1935 when he turned 70, while his mother wouldn't have qualified until 1937 when she turned 65. One day in 1938 this gentle soul met my mother Mary at a bus stop in South Shields.

As with Jack, I'm attempting to reconstruct her life from a few scattered documents and photographs in two albums. The first was compiled in haphazard fashion by her mother. The other was begun by Mary in 1938 when she was 21 and maintained through the first decade of marriage. In this album, and in a subsequent one begun in the 1950s, the photographs are neatly mounted, with captions identifying the location and date and often the dramatis personae. That was my mother's way – precise and methodical, the style of a clever, educated woman.

Hers was a turbulent spirit. After the photograph of her sat upon on her father's knee the next surviving one was taken in 1918 when she was a year old. She's seated on a cushion on a small table with Norah holding her waist to steady her. What's striking is the size of the infant's head, looking larger than her mother's. Mary inherited this big rectangular head from her maternal grandmother (after whom she was named) and her slender body from her mother. You can see the same big face in photographs as a child and as a girl and young woman. She passed on the same large head and slender body to her children. Mary kept this disproportion until her early 40s when her body thickened following a major operation that confined her to a hospital bed for over a year.

Her childhood differed from Jack's. He was the youngest child of middle-aged parents, growing up in a crowded flat surrounded by siblings growing into adults as he entered his teens. Mary was the first child of young parents, still in their mid 20s. She spent seven years as an only child. She would been her mother's helpmeet and companion while her father was at sea. Her sister Myfanwy wasn't born until 1924. The gulf in age was too big for easy companionship. Mary would always be the big sister – forceful, cleverer and more attractive, married to a handsome man and mother of two comely and spirited children. Myf never married. Ivor, born when Mary was entering her teens, was more child than sibling. Mary was raised in a superior class at a time when class was even more important than now. Jack's father ruled the dark and grimy engine room. Mary's father strode the bridge – autocrat of his maritime realm after 1927. By then Mary was living in a detached house on the edge of South Shields, with at least one servant. She attended Westoe Road School like Jack had done; but unlike him she transferred to the secondary school to study for the School Certificate. Her parents would have been able to afford the modest fee and under no pressure to push her into paid employment. Her mother's album contains photographs of her wearing a gymslip. I have a studio photograph of her as a Brownie. Our bookshelves housed a few of her favourite stories about the Chalet School in Switzerland. Aged around 12 she won a prize for scholarly prowess, awarded by the Lady Mayoress of Newcastle. Mary sits beside her in a group photograph.

Everything changed as Mary entered her teens. In 1930 home was darkened by the death of Ivor's twin Shirley. Captain Jim could no longer find a ship following the collapse in world trade. At some point in the early 1930s the family moved to Aberaeron, from which Jim's parents hailed. Today the town houses about 1,500 people. Then it was home to about 1,200. The family appear to have liked the place. In 1961, when I was 12, we visited the town, built in the early 19th century around a small harbour by a local clergyman, while on holiday in Aberystwyth in a student hall of residence run as a guest house by the Countrywide Holiday Association (CHA) during the summer vacations. My father photographed the family with his wife seated on a bench outside her former home with Vanessa and me sitting on either side.

In 1970 the Williams women were excited to see their former home, described as a "stucco building", pictured on the shilling stamp as Wales' contribution to a series showing traditional houses. All three women – Norah, Myf and my mother – made cuttings from their local newspapers, in South Shields, Birmingham and Sunderland respectively, to which they gave interviews. They were vague about the reasons for leaving South Shields for Aberaeron. None mentions Jim's inability to find a ship. Norah and Mary mention the mild climate that suited Myf's weak chest. Their home was a former coaching inn in the centre of the small town overlooking the harbour. The stamp shows the frontage and the side entrance approached beneath an arch as commonly found in coaching inns. It contained six bedrooms, a dining room and lounge, and a big kitchen with red floor-tiles. Jim bought it for £400 and christened it 'Pretty Haven'. In 1970 it was occupied by the County Planning Officer and valued at £4,000. Now it's a Grade II listed building known locally as "the stamp house".

This was where Mary finished her schooling, while Jack was still living with his parents in his boyhood home. He would have left school with the usual leaving certificate. Mary excelled in the small, single-storey county secondary school on the hillside overlooking the town. The school was opened in 1896 as an intermediary school intended to bridge the gap between the Board schools built under the 1870 Education Act and the university colleges that began to be opened during the following decades. Initially it served only 40 children taught by the head master and two assistants. By the time my mother attended in the early 1930s it had been extended twice and was serving 200 children taught by probably around ten teachers. In 1932, aged 15, Mary earned a School Certificate (precursor of O Levels and GCSEs) in Geography, French (with oral proficiency), Mathematics and Botany, with distinctions in English and History. As a boy I was entranced by the delicate watercolour sketches in her Botany exercise book, now lost. In 1934, aged 17, she earned a Higher Certificate (precursor of A Levels) in English, French ("with Conversational Power") and History. I have on my shelves one of her set books, an Everyman edition of English Essays from William Caxton to R L Stevenson inscribed by Mary Williams, Form VI, with minute, barely legible pencil annotations to essays by Charles Lamb, William Hazlitt and Thomas de Quincey. As prize for attainment she was awarded the standard history of England by G M Trevelyan.

Hers was no mean achievement. As recently as 1955, less than one in twenty pupils earned two or more A Levels. Mary told her children that she won a county scholarship for university study that she was unable to accept for the simple reason that she needed to find a job to help support the family. She, like Jack, had grown up in a world in Depression. She wanted a secure and reasonably paid job with decent prospects, just like he found. She passed the entrance exam for the Executive class in the civil service and joined the Ministry of Labour as a manager in a Labour Exchange. Around this time, as trade recovered in the run-up to war, Jim found a ship and the family returned to South Shields. By 1936, they occupied a semi-detached house, 'The Moorings', in Marina Drive, looking across the grassy Bents and the dunes to the sea. Mary told the *Sunderland Echo* in 1970 that the family was pleased to get back to urban life, but the years in Aberaeron planted a mine inside her that would explode twenty years later.

Not long after returning to South Shields Mary met my father. A photograph from that time shows her standing on the pavement in Marina Drive, wearing a white dress and grasping a tennis racket – a veritable Joan Hunter-Dunn. During the mid 1960s the NEEB closed their office in Sunderland and my father transferred to Newcastle. He would catch a bus to Sunderland station. Occasionally over dinner he would mention that some woman had struck up a conversation at the bus stop or on the bus itself. These stories embarrassed me at the time and continued to puzzle me until Vanessa said Mam had told her that she'd met Dad at a bus stop. Dad must have been reminding his wife that he was still an attractive man, even in his late 50s – like his father had been.

From all I know of my parents, Mary would have made the running. She was a clever and elegant young woman, aged 21, with a pleasant face and a trim figure. Photographs taken on holiday with friends at the local government trade union resort at Cayton Bay near Scarborough in 1937 show the girls in playful mode. The first page of her album sets the tone. One photograph shows a young man with his arms over the shoulders of Mary and another girl. The second shows Mary with three other girls on the beach. The same girls appear in photographs on subsequent pages. One of them flaunts shapely tanned legs. Another wears a halter-neck dress showing her back naked to the waist – still hot today. A third photograph shows the same girl doing a handstand with Mary holding her legs, while another girl crawls beneath the arch created by her friends. An earlier photograph from 1936 shows three sharp-suited young men. As Jon Savage remarks in his study of the emergence of the teenager: "By the end of the 1930s a separate youth culture had become part of everyday life in Britain", embracing cinemas, theatres and dance halls – and lidos, like the sea-water swimming pool north of the Groyne in South Shields, where my parents, both keen swimmers, would have displayed strong, tanned bodies. A generation before Elvis and the Beatles, Mary enjoyed this emerging youth culture, before it was cut short by war.

I've placed the only photograph of my parents from this period at the head of this chapter. Like every photograph in my mother's albums it carries a date – September 1938, during the Munich crisis, as war threatened. They're in romantic mood. Jack smiles as Mary gazes up at him. Then he seems to have disappeared from her life. What happened? After the photographs from Cayton Bay my mother's album contains several from a visit with her mother to the South of France – at that time simply the most fashionable place in the world. They might have been celebrating Mary's 21st birthday. Three photographs show a party seated around a table at the entrance to the Grand Hotel, Menton. Others show the Casino in Monte Carlo, the market place in Grasse, the yacht belonging to a once-famous lady socialite in the harbour at Menton, and a group of four women including Mary against the backdrop of the spectacular Gorge du Loup railway viaduct, dynamited by the Germans following the Allied landings in the South of France in August 1944. Suddenly we're in the world of Nancy Mitford and Noel Coward. This holiday must have made a huge impression on a South Shields girl just turned 21 – especially when she'd have had an opportunity to exercise her French conversational power.

One photograph shows an elegantly suited man, head slightly tilted, aged in his early 30s, seated on a wall outside the Grand Hotel. The same man appears in a series of photographs from 1939 outside a substantial half-timbered house labelled in the album as Poynton Manor, in Shropshire. Thanks to Mr Google I've been able to take a virtual walk around Poynton Manor, a hamlet comprising just a few dozen dwellings east of the A442 a couple of miles north of Wellington. I found no trace of the house visited by young Mary. Most of her photographs seem to have been taken on one occasion. One shows the man from Menton outside the house which he must have owned. Another looking from directly behind a big saloon car shows Mary leaning against it, with her jacket folded over her arms, while the man stands to one side facing the camera. A third shows the man standing behind Mary and another woman. The photograph at the start of the chapter must have been taken on a different occasion, as my mother's wearing a dress. This time they're arm in arm.

I'm struck by the romantic look of the photographs of my mother with Jack and this other man. I know no more about this man than I do about 'The Professor'. The photographs at Poynton are dated from 1939. At this time Mary was living with her parents in South Shields. She told me only that she parted from my father for a time and became involved with another man whom she met in France. She said more to Vanessa. One day early in the war they were planning to meet in Newcastle when he sent a curt postcard saying that he'd have to "cut" the meeting. She never heard from him again – though she kept the postcard and showed it to Vanessa. They must have known one another for around 18 months. Possibly, just possibly, he asked Mary to become his mistress and she refused – which might explain why later she would become so protective of what she'd have thought of as her daughter's virtue. Judging from the photographs, this man would have offered Mary a different life to the one she had with Jack – a more expansive one that might have suited her better. She didn't forget this man. She kept the photographs for her children to find – like Jack kept the photographs taken by 'The Professor'. Both sets of photographs show them in their early 20s, on the threshold of adult life.

Mary must have left South Shields for London soon after the end of this romance. She spent the winter of the Blitz living in Streatham and working in the Labour Exchange in Tooting. She told her children about fire-watching on the roof. Early in 1941 she returned to South Shields in poor health and got in touch with Jack. He'd joined the RAF in 1939 and was working in ground crew on one of the bomber bases in the East of England. He'd been barred from flying because of poor eye-sight and a damaged ear-drum. Otherwise, almost certainly he'd have been killed in action. He and Mary would have met during periods of home leave in South Shields. My parents never felt any doubt that Britain would prevail but they met again during the darkest period of the war. Churchill confessed in his war memoirs that he could not recall "any period [of the war] when its stresses and the onset of so many problems all at once or in rapid succession bore more directly on me and my colleagues than the first half of 1941." While Mary and Jack were getting to know one another again Britain was being defeated in short order in Greece, Crete and Libya. While the Red Army was reeling under the impact of German invasion Mary would have heard that her father's ship had been sunk. For weeks she wouldn't have known whether he was alive or dead. My father was a kind, handsome man. He was likely to survive the war and to return to a secure job. Mary was entering her mid 20s. She'd have known passion during her romance with the mysterious man from Poynton Manor. She was determined to marry. She must have decided Jack was the right man. He told me how much in awe he was of her intellect. He thought her the right woman to bear his children. They married quickly, within months, while she was waiting for her father to return from South Africa.

Mary and Jack celebrated their Golden Wedding anniversary in October 1991 surrounded by their ostensibly happily married children with their spouses and four boisterous grandsons (two for each child) produced annually between 1986 and 1989. Myf joined them and Peggie sent congratulations. Within 18 months Mary was dead from cancer. Their years together divide almost too neatly into distinct decades, highs alternating with lows.

After a week's honeymoon in Torquay, my mother would have returned to work in the Labour Exchange in South Shields. She would have lived in her parents' home in Marina Drive, where she would have introduced her new husband to her father on his return from South Africa. Jack would have gone back to the station where he serviced the twin-engined Vickers Wellingtons which formed the main strike force of Bomber Command in the early years of war. He'd work on the four-engined Avro Lancasters after they entered service in 1942. As a boy I was obsessed with the Second World War, especially the war in the air. In the photograph on page 168 you can see the RAF button that I wore in the lapel of my school blazer. I'd pump my father for stories about the war. He recalled no heroics. He'd load the bombs in the bowels of the aircraft and the ammunition belts in the machine-gun turrets. Sometimes he'd work in an underground factory assembling bombs. He saw air-crew set off for a few pints in the pub one evening and fail to return from a raid the following night. He saw crippled bombers struggle back to base, only to crash-land and explode. He spent some of his spare time filing and polishing a brass model fighter-plane, half Spitfire and half Hurricane, with which I played as a boy and now, sans propeller lost long ago, graces the window-sill of my study. Unless memory deceives, he told me that in the last weeks of the war he and other ground crew were taken in one of the bombers on a macabre joy ride over the Ruhr. He told me about the ocean of ruins beneath the plane, as shown in famous photographs of Cologne, with the cathedral blackened but still standing because, so the story goes, it afforded a superb landmark for the bombers.

Jack would have gone on leave to his wife's parents' home in Marina Drive. He'd have visited his widowed mother and his sister Peggie, both still living in South Shields. His nephew David recalled surprise visits from the young couple and wonderful Christmas presents. My mother's album is full of the photographs of early married life that all happy couples collect – wartime weekends in the Lake District that Jack loved. A photograph from 1945 shows them standing outside the pretty little house in South Shields which they bought after my father was demobilised. He returned to his job in the accounts office of the Borough Council and transferred to the new public corporation when the electricity supply industry was nationalised in 1947. He studied to qualify as a chartered municipal accountant. About this time he must have become a freemason, though later he'd ridicule the whole thing. I've always assumed that my mother had to give up her job in the Labour Exchange on account of the notorious bar on the employment of married women in public services that lasted into the 1950s. She would defend this restriction on the grounds that it opened positions for men released from the forces. She had the ability but not the ambition to make a career of her own. Marriage and family came first, as for most women of her generation. During the late 1970s, as Vanessa entered her late 20s without a husband, she wrote to me in despair that she "might end up like Myfanwy" as a single woman. She and Jack enjoyed the kind of walking holidays that they'd resume ten years later with their children, staying in guest houses in Morecambe, on the Isle of Man, at Cromer and of course in the Lake District.

You can see from my mother's photograph album that the 1940s were good years. The 1950s, as they crossed the shadow-line into middle age, weren't so good. Photographs in a new album tell their own story. My father's waist thickened. He acquired the same streak of white hair, like a badger's I thought, that his mother had in middle age. His face fell into the taciturn expression, one I've inherited, that he'd keep for the rest of his life, rarely cracking a smile for a camera. The change in my mother was harsher – from the slim, elegant young mother in the early 1950s to a dumpy matron with an old lady's thick ankles by the end of the decade. In 1952 she gave birth to Vanessa, named after the heroine of Hugh Walpole's historical romances set in the Lake District. Later she'd devour Catherine Cookson's tales of Tyneside and Winston Graham's Poldark novels. She might have enjoyed the Shipyard Girls.

In 1954 the family moved to Sunderland as I neared school age. Their marriage seems to have soured. My father stopped trying to qualify as an accountant and reconciled himself to a career as a clerk. His failure would have dismayed his clever wife, whose father had risen to master mariner. In the letter that recalled happy wartime visits, Cousin David reminded me of a notable eccentricity of my father, who "announced that he was never going to wash his hair – only brush it vigorously, in the interests of not going bald!" He kept a good head of hair (as he would have done anyway) but left dark, sticky stains on the headboard on his side of the bed and on the back of the armchair in which he sat – which must have been a trial to his wife. Eventually he began to wash his hair, and his wife acquired a new headboard and living room suite. Cousin David described my father as "a fitness freak" – not surprising after the early deaths of Winnie and Sam. Every morning before breakfast he'd drink a pint of warm water – to flush out his intestines, as he put it. I've continued the habit.

In the mid 1950s the mine that had been laid in Aberaeron exploded inside my mother, as her spine crumbled from tuberculosis contracted from drinking unpasteurised milk. In 1976 she told me how a hospital consultant warned her that "if I wanted to live I would have to lie in a plaster cast for a year or eighteen months." In July 1957 she entered hospital to undergo cutting-edge surgery, equivalent to a heart transplant a few years later, to remove diseased bone from her spine and replace it with healthy bone from her legs. She had to spend a year on her back while the bones knitted, followed by months of physiotherapy as she learned to walk again. She didn't return home until summer 1958. The operation saved her life but ravaged her body and her looks.

The 1960s were better. Adversity restored my parents' marriage. My father had taken good care of the chicks while his wife was in hospital. After she'd recovered health and strength, and I'd entered Bede Grammar School, she went back to work, first for a couple of days in a mail order despatching centre, and later for more days as a Clerical Officer in the local office of the Department of Health and Social Security. One task was to assess clients' claims for benefits – in which she took pride as a stern custodian of public money. She attended one or two promotion boards but never managed to regain the position of Executive Officer which she'd once held. Her earnings helped to pay for a second-hand Hillman Minx and a series of holidays of the kind my parents had enjoyed as a young couple. In 1967, as I was about to sit my A Level exams, we moved to a bigger semi-detached house near the Bede. Two of Sunderland's footballers (including the celebrated Jimmy Montgomery who'd keep goal against Leeds in the momentous Cup Final victory in 1973) lived in the same road – which says more about the earnings of professional footballers in those days than my parents' income. My father ploughed on at the NEEB, earning a silver pocket watch for 25 years service and then the gold watch that I'm wearing. I left for university in 1967. Vanessa left school after O Levels in 1969 and left Sunderland to work as a hotel manager in Leeds in 1972. We'd long grown beyond our mother's command.

During the 1960s I noticed the tension between my father and his mother- and sister-in-law – Little Gran and Auntie Myf. He sought to recruit me to his side by snide comments. He discovered that the surest way to annoy me was to say I looked like Ivor. As I grew older I began to be troubled by this behaviour. I suspect it went back to the early years of the marriage, while Mary was still living at home. When I studied D H Lawrence's *Sons and Lovers* for A Level English I concluded that it was provoked by what

Richard Sennett and Jonathan Cobb called "the hidden injuries of class" in their book of that title, published in 1972. My mother was a clever middle-class woman who'd married a less educated man of humbler origins. My father could be proletarian in his habits – bending the blade of his knife to sup gravy from his plate, blowing his nose with his fingers – and childishly petulant – for example when disappointed by a Christmas present or a meal that displeased him. As a young married man he must have endured petty humiliations – "micro-aggressions" some would call them now – from Norah and Myf. His mother-in-law might have thought that her daughter had married beneath her. In old age Myf found significance in the way Mary and Jack had married before her father returned from South Africa. I could find no record in my diary but I recall one family gathering in my teens or student years when my father mimicked Myf's manner of speech and quarrelled with Norah who sprang to her defence. They left abruptly. For a while my father refused to allow them in the house. He refused to drive my mother to South Shields, so she had to take a bus to visit her mother. On occasion, after I'd learned to drive, I acted as chauffeur. In his last years my father told me he regretted his conduct. He described Norah as a brave woman and had kind words for Myf.

I was starting to understand my parents as people and not just Mam and Dad. Both were religious, my father in a vague non-denominational Protestant way. He bought the vividly illustrated Bunyan that captivated me. He kept a few slim volumes of inspirational reading by his bedside. After he died I found a notebook with handwritten prayers for various occasions. My mother was confirmed in the Church of England. She kept the *New English Bible* by her bedside. In the early 1960s they attended the local Anglican church of St Nicholas (which ran a popular youth club). For a year or two my father ran one its Sunday School classes. I attended another but found no inspiration, despite managing to win a pretty little *Book of Common Prayer* in a diocesan competition. I felt the vicar awarded it with some exasperation. He must have realised that I was (in Max Weber's famous phrase) "religiously 'unmusical'". I chose to indulge my mother by attending confirmation class at Christ Church and was duly confirmed when I was 14. Vanessa did not. I don't think I ever took Communion, though I have on my shelves the King James Bible that Little Gran bought me for Christmas in 1957, along with my father's Bunyan and the little Prayer Book. During personal troubles in 1973, both parents besought me to find comfort in religion. Theirs was a practical religion. After they retired from work in 1975 he drove for Meals on Wheels and then volunteered for Citizens Advice, while she served in the shop at the Royal Infirmary in Durham Road. They went on pilgrimage to Oberammergau in 1980. She was disappointed never to visit the Holy Land. In her last years she attended the local parish church as long as she was able, and her funeral was well attended. Her ashes (and then his) were interred in the church yard.

My mother's strongest passion, though, was not for religion but for politics. In a list of interests compiled in the 1980s she placed politics ahead of literature, drama, opera and the church (in that order). She might have been a staunch monarchist but she held a sternly republican view of politics that would have been applauded by Aristotle or Machiavelli – active engagement as part of the duty of a citizen. Her father's stories from his voyages and her love of history must have awakened her interest. The Depression would have shown how global forces can affect individual lives. She told me she'd supported the Republicans in the Spanish Civil War; and her father's liking for China must have led her to sympathise with its struggle against Japan. She thought war with Germany was bound to come. In the 1960s she canvassed for Conservative candidates. In 1969 she led a campaign against a new leisure centre full of gaming machines. In 1971 she persuaded my father to accompany her to Newcastle for meetings of the Monday Club which supported Enoch Powell in his campaign against Commonwealth immigration, leaving after it was infiltrated by the National Front. In the early 1970s she stood unsuccessfully for the Conservatives in council elections. In 1974 she led the Sunderland Rent and Ratepayers' Association that submitted evidence to the Committee on Local Government Finance on whose secretariat I was working in my first job as a civil servant. Of course she admired Margaret Thatcher, until doubts set in over the Poll Tax in 1990. By then my parents were living in a small flat in Surrey, to which they'd moved to be close to Vanessa. My mother wondered why she and Jack should pay the same local tax as Vanessa and her husband in their big detached house.

My father took his lead from his wife. As a student I asked about his political views in the 1930s, expecting him to have shared my mother's sympathies. Even when pressed he couldn't recall having taken much interest. He'd grown up in decent poverty. His instincts were on the left. As a student I used to recommend books that I thought he'd enjoy, like Robert Tressell's *The Ragged-Trousered Philanthropists* about house-painters in Hastings, and autobiographies of socialist pioneer Robert Owen and Thomas Cooper the Chartist. He thought Friedrich Engels' *Condition of the Working Class in England in 1844* "should be compulsory reading for everyone". In a letter in June 1969 he looked forward to a reduction in working hours over the next 50 years which would allow more time for what he called, in a phrase redolent of Morecambe and Wise (and Stevie Wonder), "the sunshine of life". He'd voted Labour in 1945 and did so again in 1964, but by the late 1970s he supported Mrs Thatcher with as much enthusiasm as his wife. They switched from *The Sunday Times* to *The Telegraph* and relished Peregrine Worsthorne's pieces (sometimes sent on to me).

My father's passions were for sport and music. Photographs of him as young man show a strong athletic body. I believe he played rugby and cricket and he swam and cycled. He passed on his love of country walking to his children. In the late 1960s my mother encouraged him to take up golf. In 1982 he told his sceptical son how he'd "enjoyed lots of golf, & find myself hitting some lovely shots. To non-golfers this may seem a futile joy but it is such a thrill that a good round sometimes keeps me awake thinking about it." In his last years he'd spend hours in front of the television watching sport

– any sport, even snooker and darts (both enjoying a heyday in those years). He loved the poems he'd encountered when young. He would quote Kipling. He introduced me as a boy to Robert Browning's 'The Pied Piper of Hamelin' ("Great rats, small rats, lean rats, brawny rats, / Brown rats, black rats, grey rats, tawny rats, / Grave old plodders, gay young friskers") and Alfred Lord Tennyson's 'The Revenge' ("At Flores, in the Azores, Sir Richard Grenville lay, / And a pinnace, like a flutter'd bird, came flying from far away; / 'Spanish ships of war at sea! We have sighted fifty-three!'"). Every spring he'd learn Browning's 'Home Thoughts from Abroad': "Oh, to be in England / Now that April's there". He liked sentimental songs by Kenneth MacKellar. He bought Shirley Bassey's 'I (who have nothing)' – perhaps he felt the lyrics contained some echo of his complex emotions for his wife. Vanessa and I grew up in homes with an upright piano in our small living rooms. He paid for lessons for both of us, though neither persevered and the piano was sold when we moved house in 1967. When clearing the garage I found the second-hand violin which he struggled unsuccessfully to play. I've given it a good home with my son David's musician wife. I believe Norman ("The Professor") encouraged him to perform in amateur productions of Gilbert & Sullivan. In his 60s he sang in the amateur chorus of a professional production of *Der Rosenkavalier* at the Sunderland Empire. He shared my mother's love for opera. *La Traviata* and *La Boheme* were favourites. One Sunday in his last years we drove to Chelmsford to visit my sister-in-law's family. He sat on the back seat between my small sons while I played Neil Young's 'Unplugged' album. He was in tears when we arrived.

The 1970s seem to have begun well. Both parents were in good health and still earning. I took my last holiday with them in 1966. Vanessa accompanied them for another year or two. From 1970 they took part in the sudden increase in Britons enjoying package holidays in Spain, Italy and Yugoslavia, up from 4 million in 1971 to 9 million in 1973. I have photographs of them striding out one evening in 1971 in Cattolica near Rimini, tanned and happy, with my father cracking a rare smile caught on camera. My mother loved the sun, despite coming out in millions of freckles. I wish I could find the photograph of her, perhaps from Cattolica, sitting in a bikini on the patio of their apartment. But they worried about my career prospects until I won a position in the civil service – a nice safe job with good prospects. They had barely regained equilibrium when Vanessa's decision to live with a man outside of marriage brought my mother to the brink of mental breakdown. "We just can't understand", she told me in June 1976, taking for granted her husband's agreement, "how any single young woman, brought up in a decent, respectable home, where the parents at least tried to live by Christian principles, could live openly with a man as his wife, especially when there are no obstacles, financial or otherwise to their marriage." For a time, I believe, she hardly slept. I was glad when she told me that I'd helped her "to see things in perspective". After all, she said, I'd lived the same kind of life. But then I was a man, which made it OK. In 1979 she chose to "pause" relations with Vanessa until she found a husband. My father felt he had to stand by his wife but told me "[b]etween you and me, that Vanessa should do what she wants, and she should have a good idea how to weigh up the prospects for the future." Sadly he seemed unable to help his wife to overcome what she described as "three years of darkness".

Meanwhile my father's health deteriorated after he retired in 1975. Trouble with his knees prevented him from playing as much golf as he'd once done. What I thought had been dullness in company was caused by growing deafness resulting from damage to his eardrums as a young man. He required hearing aids in both ears and was prone to drop out of conversation. He began to be troubled with angina. I had to slow my pace when we went for walk. He fell into a grump when my parents visited my flat in London one afternoon in 1978 and I served tea and cakes when he'd been expecting a cooked meal. My mother struggled to pacify him.

I heard occasional sounds of love-making in the bedroom beside mine when I was home from university in the late 1960s, but I gathered from Vanessa that sexual relations ceased during the 1970s. Photographs from early married life show a strong physical connection. But an educated woman must have been disappointed by her husband's failure to qualify as an accountant. By the mid 1950s my mother must have been suffering increasing back pain, probably aggravated by child-birth and house-keeping without labour-saving devices. She confided in Vanessa that around this time she developed feelings for a neighbour. After she returned from 15 months in hospital she must have hated the changes in her body. She'd never look elegant again. She probably struggled to feel desirable. She can't have liked her husband's treatment of her mother and sister. There were those odd little conversations at dinner. My father would respond in a passive-aggressive fashion if my mother made any change in culinary routine: one evening she cooked spaghetti Bolognese and he spent half an hour eating it with his knife and fork. He told Vanessa after the death of my mother that he thought he'd always loved her more than she'd loved him, and that he might have been happier if he'd stayed with a woman near his air-base whom he'd been seeing in 1941 when Mary got back in touch.

Life brightened during their last decade. Vanessa re-entered our mother's good books after she met the man she'd marry in 1981. I recall a happy family Christmas in their first home in West London. By Christmas 1982 I'd met the woman whom I'd marry in October 1983. Our mother compiled long and detailed accounts of both weddings. Photographs from the account of mine show a bustling, happy presence in a light blue suit and a large hat – while my father presented his usual taciturn visage. In 1984, with babies on the horizon, my parents sold their house in Sunderland and bought a small flat, all they could afford, in Sunninghill, a short drive from Vanessa's new home in Datchet, across the river from Windsor. Babies began to arrive in 1986 – four grandsons by the time of their Golden Wedding anniversary in 1991. The following year my mother contracted pancreatic cancer, which brought her a swift death in March 1993. As she lay dying she confided in me and my wife that my father had been a good husband even though she hadn't always appreciated him.

For the first time my father, aged 82, had to manage on his own. Following the end of Vanessa's marriage in 1994 he could no longer find comfort in cosy weekends in a family home. Around this time he had to give up on golf after a minor car accident in which he'd been at fault. Soon he was unable even to get out for a walk. At last he could no longer take care of himself and his home. After his death I received a letter from my mother's girlhood friend Eveline, now aged around 80, crippled by arthritis and with her husband Jim (a former sea captain) sinking into dementia. She'd known my father since they were young. They kept in touch after my mother's death and would talk over the phone a few times a year. "I know how very lonely he was", she wrote, "after all their years together. The last time I spoke to him he seemed very down when he wasn't able to go for his usual walks any more he did miss those." He became unaccountably angry one day when I drove over to see him with my sons.

By 1998 he'd reached the point when Vanessa and I decided that he would have to enter a care home. He anticipated us with a massive stroke during the night before we planned to tell him. He never awakened, and died in hospital a few days later. Big sister Peggie outlived him by a year. At his funeral, as I'd done at my mother's, I read Bunyan's account of Christian crossing the River of death to the City of everlasting life. My older son David, aged 11, insisted on attending the funeral, with his mother and me and Vanessa. He listened to my eulogy and my reading, and chose to read the same passage at Myf's funeral.

Chapter 5

Non Serviam

A man who has been the indisputable favourite of his mother keeps for life the feeling of a conqueror.

(Sigmund Freud, 'A Childhood Recollection from [Goethe's] *Dichtung und Wahrheit*,' 1917)

It is right to rebel.

(Mao Zedong, 'A Letter to the Red Guards of Tsinghua University Middle School,' 1 August 1966)

The cover shows one of the photographs taken at Infants' schools I attended in Sunderland between 1954 and 1956. In all of them I'm wearing a cardigan or sweater open at the neck to show collar and tie. My hair's cut short – probably by my father as I hated visiting the barber's. I'm looking straight at the camera. In three of the shots I've got my lower lip drawn behind my upper teeth, with a sly smile, as though I've something to hide.

That's how I must have looked one Monday in 1955 when, aged 6, I set off to walk a mile or so to Fulwell Infants' School in Sea Road. The lower photograph opposite must have been taken a few years earlier. I can spot my home in the street running parallel to the road behind Roker Park. Home was a small semi-detached house at 38 Park Lea Road built in Edwardian times. Fulwell School had been built in 1890 by Sunderland School Board – the same year as Westoe Road School attended by my parents. I'd already spent a year at Redby Infants' School built in 1899 on Fulwell Road near the back of the photograph. Fulwell School is outside the photograph to the right. I spent three years in the same kind of Board School, rising above the neighbouring streets, with the same high windows and asphalt playground, as my parents had done.

On that day in 1955 my mother might have watched me turn left and walk northwards along the road as on any other morning. I'd continue past my friend John Singer's family bungalow on the corner, across Side Cliff Road and along Mere Knolls Road before turning left into Sea Road. This was the main local thoroughfare, lined with small shops and graced by the elegant Art Deco-styled Marina cinema where I'd attend the Kids Club on Saturday mornings. Today, though, I had other plans. Once I was sure my mother wasn't watching I'd have crossed Park Lea Road and turned right into North Grove leading towards Roker Park and the sea. The landowner had donated the land for the park as part of a deal opening the area for housing, under which the council built the coast road, including the bridge spanning the ravine running down to the sea.

From North Grove I'd have crossed Roker Park Road and taken a few steps along the pavement before turning into the park. I knew it well. Grandpa Jim had bought me a small yacht that I'd sail in the boating lake. Once I'd fallen in, probably while reaching for the yacht. On this morning I'd have walked in the other direction, past two bowling-greens. I'd have turned right, past the octagonal cast-iron bandstand and down the path through the ravine to the sea front. As I entered the ravine I might have glanced at the fairy dell built into the slope on my right. I'd have seen the dell, with the ravine and bandstand, illuminated in the autumn. As the ravine deepened I'd have walked under a footbridge and then the road bridge forty or fifty feet above my head. As the path widened, I'd have stepped into Marine Walk, with the beach in front of me. My walk would have taken no more than 15 minutes. I'd done it scores of times but today I was playing truant.

Obviously I've no idea how I spent the hours when I should have been in school. I'd have found plenty to occupy myself. Ahead was the beach. To my right along Marine Walk I could walk towards the mouth of the River Wear embraced by piers extending almost a mile out to sea. Once past the base of the north pier I probably would have shunned the beach that was never adequately cleansed by the tide and walked on to a smaller pier at the mouth of the river. From this vantage point I could have watched the ships passing in and out of a busy port. Alternatively I might have ascended the long ramp from Marine Walk to the coastal road and the Bungalow Cafe with its sign pointing over the sea to Germany. From there I might have walked down to the inner pier or round towards the North Dock, with a railway and timber yards on my right. I could look upriver to the shipyards and hear the clang of shipbuilding.

When weary of ships and shipbuilding I could have retraced my steps along Marine Walk and past the exit from the ravine. If the tide was low I could have walked onto a sandy beach and continued round a cliff and along another stretch of sand towards the Cat and Dog Steps. By local legend this was the spot where once upon a time dead cats and dogs washed in with the tide. Since the 1930s a wide concrete ramp had formed the start of a promenade to Seaburn half a mile away. This was the most popular part of the beach. Families would throng here at high tide on a sunny day, enjoying the suntrap formed by the concrete ramp and the cliff behind it. I'd spent many days with my parents and Vanessa, with my friends and their parents, paddling and building canals from pool to pool and dams against the tide. One day in 1996 when I visited the North East for the first time since the early 1980s I took photographs of my sons, aged 9 and 6, playing self-consciously on the sand in front of the Cat and Dog Steps. Forty-one years earlier, at the same age as my younger son, I might have climbed the narrow Steps to Cliff Park. I'd have walked by the lighthouse and the round red-painted reclaimed mine with a slot for pennies for the Shipwrecked Mariners Society. If the tide was high I would have continued along the promenade. Otherwise, I would have made my way across an expanse of sand and rocks, investigating pools exposed by the ebbing tide.

At Seaburn I might have visited the amusement park or simply wandered along another stretch of beach towards Whitburn village where the Rev Charles Lutwidge Dodgson (Lewis Carroll) had taken his holidays. By local legend he found inspiration while walking the sands for 'The Walrus and the

Carpenter': "The Walrus and the Carpenter / Were walking close at hand: / They wept like anything to see / Such quantities of sand." Sunderland Museum acquired its famous stuffed walrus after the poem was written, but the Rev Dodgson might have seen a different specimen in the home of his brother-in-law, another clergyman, in Southwick on the northern bank of the Wear near the present Stadium of Light. In this small boy's paradise I'd have had no difficulty in finding things to do.

My mother was no fool. I wonder how I managed to avoid arousing her suspicion. I must have arrived home for lunch and tea at the usual times. I might have owned a wrist-watch, though I wouldn't have needed one. I could have checked clocks on the seafront, or popped into a shop or cafe to glance at a clock; or I could have simply asked a passing grown-up: "please Mister, can you tell me the time?" Suffice to say that I managed to deceive my mother on Monday and Tuesday. On Wednesday I set off with my usual plans for a day by the sea. When I returned, either at lunch-time or for tea, my mother asked where I'd been. I must have claimed to have been at school, because I've never forgotten her reply: "No, you haven't, Michael – because I've had the school attendance officer here and you haven't been to school this week."

I would have told my mother about my troubles with Miss Elliot, the headmistress. I've discovered through Facebook that she was a tall, thin, stern woman, who might soften when listening to a child read. She was approaching retirement by this time. She would have been born in the 1890s. Perhaps she'd lost a sweetheart or husband in the First World War and devoted her life to the education of other people's children – like tens of thousands of bereaved women of her generation. I must have provoked her. She must have decided that the right punishment was to demote me from one class to another. I would have accepted a rap on the knuckles without demur, but perhaps she'd tried the ruler already. Demotion must have offended my small boy's sense of justice. I wasn't going to be sat among the dunces, the stupid rough children. I decided to resist in the only way

I could, by skipping school. I must have seen no point in complaining to my mother and asking her to intercede. I'd been naughty and would have expected her to be as angry as Miss Elliot. I might have recalled how angry she'd been when she and my father turned up to see me in a Nativity Play after I'd failed to tell them I'd been removed for misbehaviour. I must have felt I had no option but to act alone.

Modern readers will puzzle over how a loving mother could allow her small son to walk a mile or so to and from school on his own, crossing several streets. That was what we did. The streets would have been full of children walking to and from school. Main thoroughfares like Sea Road were lined with shops. Housewives shopped daily before they owned fridges. There must have been only a few more cars than before the war. I was able to spend three school days roaming miles of sea-front without an adult molesting me or asking what I was doing. I'm struck by how self-sufficient I was at such a young age, able to occupy myself happily for three days. This was a society in which children inhabited their own worlds for much of the time.

I can't remember what happened next. Once she'd come to terms with my dissimulation, my mother would have appreciated that I had reason to feel aggrieved. She would have escorted me to school and made my case to Miss Elliot. She probably extracted promises of improved behaviour. All I recall is that I was released from the punishment battalion and restored to my original class. I'd stood my ground against an adult. I'd rebelled, and I'd prevailed.

I was too young to describe what I'd learned from this episode but if I'd been able I'd have drawn two conclusions. First would have been Bunyan's lesson that you had to be prepared to stand your ground, if necessary alone. Second would have been that however small and weak, you might still be able to prevail, even against apparently powerful opposition, so long as you had right on your side. Few people even then would have justified the way Miss Elliot treated one class as a punishment battalion for recalcitrants from another. But the past is another country, where people did things differently.

By the time of my truancy the family had been living in Park Lea Road for a couple of years, after moving from South Shields where I'd been born in January 1949 – just about the peak of the post-war baby boom. I wasn't the first son but I was the first to live – and all the more precious for that reason. One day my mother told me the name of the boy who was strangled at birth by her umbilical cord. I think it was Nigel. I was given the second name John after my father – like Vanessa would be given the second name Margaret after his mother and sister.

My parents took me home to 18 Harton Rise in South Shields where they'd lived since 1945. I've described it as a pretty little Edwardian semi-detached cottage, with leaded casement windows and a bow-window on the ground floor, fronted by a small garden bounded by a wooden fence and gate – built around the same time and in similar style to the terraced house in Rookfield Garden Village at the foot of Muswell Hill to which I would bring home my own first-born son and his mother almost 40 years later. Now my first home has lost its front garden to a car port, and the wooden doors and windows have been replaced with PVC fittings. Otherwise it's in pretty good shape, like the rest of the street.

Harton Rise stands about a mile from the sandy main beach and not much further from stony Marsden beach. When my parents bought their first home in 1945 it must have been near the edge of town, with only fields separating it from the coast road. By the time we moved to Sunderland in 1953 houses had spread across the fields. Beyond the coast road little has changed since the 1950s. The beach between the pier and Trow Rocks is much the same. South from Trow Rocks the grassy Leas above the cliffs stretch south to Marsden, with its spectacular rock outcrop to which children can wade at low tide. In 1949 my mother's parents were still living in Marina Drive. Nearby was an amusement park, and beyond it the sinuous pier framing the mouth of the Tyne with its companion on the northern shore. My father and I would walk beyond the pier to the stumpy Groyne for a good view of the Fish Quay in North Shields where trawlers would unload their catches. We could watch colliers steaming in and out of the Tyne, and ferries to and from Norway. Here I spent my first years, in a busy port with a pretty sea-side which my parents had known as children. I'd spend days on the beach, in Marine Park with my mother, or walking the Leas with my father.

I can think myself back to this angel infancy with the help of a tan-coloured album, with the gold-embossed words "Baby" on the cover, given to my mother by Auntie Myf. The first few pages record my developmental progress followed by pages of photographs of my early years before Vanessa was born. No mother could have kept a more comprehensive and meticulous record than did mine. She noted the timing of all key stages in physical development, from holding up my head to walking, and the days when I cut each one of my baby teeth. She recorded my weight once a week for six months and at gradually longer intervals for three years until Vanessa arrived, when she started keeping the same record for her – albeit not in quite the same detail. She charted my acquisition of basic social skills, from first smile to first dry night. Neither my first sentence – 'Engine go 'long there' – nor my first nursery rhyme – 'Little Miss Moffet' – escaped attention. The record ends in November 1952: "first party alone – Tony Trzoska, 3, Harton Rise – great success." I had entered society.

The photographs were mounted with the same meticulous care. Date and location and dramatis personae are recorded in minute detail. In her concern for accuracy my mother even corrected my age in two photographs. There I am in each of them – a flaxen-haired, neatly turned-out, smiling little boy. In the earliest, from 1949 and 1950, I'm in a big pram or being held up by or sitting with one or other parent, or with my mother's family – apart from two with Big Gran. By 1951 I'm toddling in the garden or playing with toys or running along a path in a park. During my first holiday at Cayton Bay, where my mother had holidayed before the war, I'm seated on her knee in vest and pants after, as she described the occasion, I'd "ventured into the sea & after a few mins sat down in all his clothes." How many small children must have done the same on their first encounter with the sea? In another photograph from that holiday I'm standing among a group of other children in a coat that seems several sizes too big.

Now I'm touching the borders of memory. I hated that coat. As an economy my mother would buy clothes for me to "grow into" – which I had done by 1952 judging from a photograph taken then. In a second photograph from that summer I'm standing in the garden with my arms round Michael and Tony Trzoska, sons of Polish exiles. Another shows me sitting on a child's saddle on the crossbar of my father's bike. That's something else I recall. By this time I was playing in the streets. One friend had a bow and arrows and fired into my mouth. No harm was done. This was a normal hazard of children's play. In two photographs from Christmas Day 1952 I'm standing beside a tricycle which must have been my main present, and then standing with two friends, David and Alan, both two or three years older. My father liked to tell how these lads, and the Trzoskas, would watch me at work on a jigsaw and exclaim: "Eeeh, Mr Williams, look at little Michael." Looking back from 1979 he recalled my "genius for jigsaws". I recall an early battle of wills with my mother. She'd prepared a bowl of sliced bananas as a treat. I refused to eat them. I hated the taste, texture and smell, and still do. She refused to allow me to leave the table until I'd eaten the fruit she'd prepared. In the end I prevailed – as children usually do in this kind of contest. Even now I'll remove fragments of banana from a bowl of muesli or fruit salad. For years I was a fussy eater. I wouldn't eat fatty meat or white bread. My father would induce me to eat mashed potato by cutting it into small squares for my fork.

We must have moved to Park Lea Road in Roker in the summer of 1953, in time to begin school around my fifth birthday. This house was a bigger version of the one in Harton Rise, built around the same time in the same style, with the same leaded casement windows, this time with stained glass in the upper portion, and a small shelf of tiles above the front door and bow window. Like the house in Harton Rise, this one has acquired a car port and PVC door and windows, though the small leaded window by the front door survives. We lived in Park Lea Road for less than three years but it's the favourite among my childhood homes. I liked living near a park and only 15 minutes from the beach. My mother was still the slender, elegant woman I see in the studio photograph from 1954 that I've placed at the head of this chapter.

My bedroom was at the rear, looking westwards. Above my bed was a small reproduction of a painting by Margaret Tarrant of angels and birds and animals around the crib of baby Jesus: "Let everything that hath breath praise the Lord." I recall lightening evenings in spring as I lay quietly in bed listening to birdsong. I'd ride my tricycle to local shops until it was stolen. Not far away stood St Andrew's Church – an Arts and Crafts masterpiece built just before the First World War to serve the newly-built suburb. Nikolas Pevsner visited in the early 1950s and described it as "without doubt one of the half-dozen best churches of its time in this country". More important was the shop owned by Alex Hastings, Captain of Sunderland football team in the 1930s, on the corner of Seaburn Terrace by the seafront. There my father bought my first toy soldiers – a set of four Confederate infantrymen, comprising three riflemen with fixed bayonets and an officer brandishing a pistol – manufactured and hand-painted for Britain's. Another favourite destination was Notorianni's ice-cream parlour, round the corner on the sea front. On the way to Whitburn village were the amusement park (with the Big Dipper erected in 1955) and a miniature railway and boating lake (all gone). The area was full of delights for children. I've sometimes described Sunderland facetiously as England's answer to Barcelona: a port and industrial town with a seaside that charmed L S Lowry as it had done Lewis Carroll – and a parish church to rival Gaudi's florid La Sagrada Familia in its modest way. Port and industry might have gone but St Andrew's remains, by the sea and not far from the Wear.

By 1953 I'd crossed the border of memory. I recall radio reports of Edmund Hillary and 'Sherpa' Tensing's ascent of Everest that coincided with the Coronation. I received one of the famous models of the Coronation coach that made the reputation of Lesney, manufacturers of the Matchbox model vehicles that rivalled the larger Dinky toys. I acquired my share of both over the next decade. I recall my father taking me to watch circus elephants parading from Monkwearmouth station along Roker Avenue and then to see them perform under the Big Top on Seaburn Recreation field. My mother would take me on shopping expeditions to the town centre. We'd catch the tram on Roker Avenue, rattling across the bridge to Fawcett Street. If an adult was standing she'd oblige me, under protest, to vacate my seat beside her and jostle with the big people in the aisle. A high point in these visits was to watch (and hear) the cash whizz away through the vacuum pipes in Blackett's, one of several department stores (all long gone).

Around this time my mother introduced me to the joys of cinema. Vanessa must have slept contentedly – unless she was at home with my father. One favourite was *Knights of the Round Table* – inspiration for *Monty Python and the Holy Grail* and *Spamalot*. There's a video on YouTube with the knights bouncing up and down on their mighty steeds. I recall the scene in which Arthur's Christian warriors set fire to dry grass to destroy the pagan Picts charging at them. My mother loved this kind of historical romance and infected me with her love of history. Another favourite was *Calamity Jane*. How could I resist Doris Day singing 'The Deadwood Stage' as it a-rolled on over a back-projected plain?

I attended two schools while living in Park Lea Road. First was Redby Infants, that's now been demolished and replaced by a modern Academy School. On my first day in 1954 my mother walked with me to school rather less than a mile away and then returned home. At the morning break I assumed school was over and walked home. My mother walked me back. For some reason I was removed from Redby and transferred to Fulwell Infants about a mile in the opposite direction. I've told all I can recall of that school, which still survives. Both must have been forbidding to a small boy.

My mother was a staunch monarchist. One of Michael Young's interviewees from the East End described her boy as: "Just the same age as Prince Charles". My mother might have said the same. Vanessa was born just a year or two after Anne. When clearing the garage I found one of my father's superfluous accountancy exercise books which my mother had repurposed as a scrapbook in which she pasted cuttings of the royal family from the early 1950s. I inherited newspapers covering every royal event between George V's Silver Anniversary in 1935 and Charles and Diana's wedding. This was one enthusiasm that my mother failed to pass on to me. I've kept the scrapbook for what it tells of her, but I asked a charity shop to find a home for the special editions. I can trace my life-long republicanism to this time. Search YouTube and you'll find newsreel of the Queen's visit to the North East in 1954. Norah and Myf had visited London for the Coronation in 1953. My mother wouldn't have wanted to miss an opportunity to see the Queen when she visited Sunderland. I complained vociferously as I stood on the pavement along the route with my mother and Vanessa (probably sheltered in her pram or push-chair) in the October wind and rain for what seemed like, and might have been, hours, waiting to catch a few seconds' glimpse of Her Majesty waving from a limousine.

My father didn't share his wife's monarchism. I recall him describing with relish over dinner one evening how he'd seen the stately Queen Mother break into a run to avoid being hit by a car while crossing the road (perhaps it was Bridge Street) during a visit to Sunderland in the 1960s. He had a taste for *schadenfreude*; he enjoyed others' discomfort. That must explain why he liked 'The Walrus and the Carpenter', especially the lines about the oysters. My father loved to recall the time when he took me and my closest friend John Singer, from the bungalow on the corner of Park Lea Road, to see *The Wizard of Oz* as a birthday treat – probably in 1955, when I was 6. I loved the film, but poor John, a year younger, was terrified by the Wicked Witch of the West. When she appeared he'd cry: "Mr Williams, Mr Williams, I want a wee-wee". My father would escort him to the toilet. I liked this story as much as he did. It reinforced my sense of self as a robust little boy. While walking along Park Lea Road in September 2021 I met a long-time resident who told me that John had died early from alcoholism, after a career as a teacher.

With a mother like mine I must have learned to read at an early age, perhaps before I entered school. Among my father's papers I found a card that I'd made for Mummy's 38th birthday in May 1955 inscribed in neat carefully-formed hand-writing. I enjoyed Noddy and Thomas the Tank Engine stories. I might have already opened my father's *Pilgrim's Progress* and found the story of Christian's battle with Apollyon. I acquired a passion for what were innocently described as Red Indians from a child's edition of Longfellow's narrative poem 'Hiawatha', almost certainly a gift from Little Gran. I was entranced by the romance of Indian life before the coming of the White Man, and gripped by the tom-tom rhythm of the verse: "Thus was born my Hiawatha, / Thus was born the child of wonder; / But the daughter of Nokomis, / Hiawatha's gentle mother. / In her anguish died deserted / By the West-Wind, false and faithless, / by the heartless Mudjekewis." Other boys might have asked for cowboy outfits and toy guns but I wanted to be an Indian with a bow and arrows. A photograph taken in August 1956 outside the front door of our new home shows me (aged 7) in Indian outfit with a feathered head-dress and brandishing a bow, with a shy Vanessa (almost 4) kitted out as Annie Oakley.

Years later I read a set of interviews with the Hungarian Communist Georg Lukacs in which he described how he acquired the same love for Indians (when he was rather older than me) after reading Fennimore Cooper's The *Last of the Mohicans* (which of course I read as well). He'd also loved *The Iliad* (which I never managed to finish).

> I learned from these two books that success is not the true criterion [of right action] and that it is the failures that are in the right [odd from a Marxist]. This emerged even more clearly in The Last of the Mohicans than in the Iliad because the Indians who had been conquered and oppressed were manifestly in the right, and not the Europeans.

Jon Savage remarks that American Indians become a symbol of individual freedom for Europeans in the early 20th century: "Despite the fact that they actually got the worst of their fictional battles with cowboys, 'redskins' were wild and free." That must have been why I liked 'Hiawatha'.

Lukacs is a prime example of the intellectual in politics. Son of a Jewish banker from Budapest, by 1914 he'd earned distinction as a philosopher and literary theorist of the most recondite kind. He's reputed to have revived interest in Soren Kierkegaard who'd been forgotten after his death in 1855. When Austria-Hungary fell apart at the end of the First World War Lukacs joined the Bolsheviks and became one of the leaders of the short-lived Hungarian Soviet Republic in 1919. After it was crushed he spent the next decades in exile in Moscow, lying low during the Great Terror, before returning to Hungary in the baggage train of the Red Army in 1945. During the 1956 Uprising he filled the same position in Imre Nagy's government as he'd done as Commissar for Education in 1919. There's a story that when Soviet forces arrested him along with other members of Nagy's government they asked him to give up his weapons and he offered his pen. It deserves to be true. He gave the long interview about his life not long before he died in 1971. At Sussex University I was taught political philosophy by one of Lukacs' star students, Istvan Meszaros, who'd fled Hungary in 1956.

The 1950s were the last in Hollywood's Golden Age, before every home acquired a television. Until then people relied on cinema and radio. During the mid 1950s my mother took me to see *Quentin Durward* (released in 1955 and set in 15th century France), *Storm over the Nile* (also from 1955 and set during Kitchener's conquest of the Sudan in 1898), *Reach for the Sky* (about Douglas Bader, who served as a fighter pilot in the Battle of Britain despite losing both legs in a flying accident) and *The Ten Commandments* (the kind of quasi-religious "spectacular" she loved), both from 1956. The film that made the biggest impression, though, was *The Vagabond King*, released in the same year and the kind of romantic tosh that my mother loved. It's based on the life of the poet Francois Villon and set in Paris in the middle of the

15th century during war between the Kings of France and the Dukes of Burgundy. My mother would have known about Villon from her Higher Certificates in French and History.

I'd forgotten the name of the film. All I could recall were a melody and a summons to "sons of toil and danger". I consulted Mr Google and found 'The Song of the Vagabonds'. Look for the YouTube video and you'll find what caught my imagination. You'll see the actor playing Francois Villon, now forgotten but then renowned for his rousing tenor, dressed in tights and doublet, with an adoring woman on his arm in a tavern full of scallywags, all in garish technicolor. He begins to sing: "Come all you Beggars of Paris town / You lousy rabble of low degree... / You and I are good for nothing but to die / We can die for Liberty." The music swells and the chorus begins: "Sons of toil and danger / Will you serve a stranger / And bow down to Burgundy." Our romantic lead draws his sword: "Onward, onward! Swords against the foe /...Sons of France around us / Break the chains that bound us / And to Hell with Burgundy." The scallywags grab swords and spears from a pair of convenient barrels and charge out of the tavern and into the streets to confront the foe. I've never forgotten that summons to "sons of toil and danger" and the sheer glamour of revolt. Of course it's all a load of total tosh but no sillier than Star Wars or Harry Potter. It captured my imagination as a seven-year-old.

In 1956 I was awakened to the drama of world politics by the simultaneous assault on Egypt by Britain, France and Israel, and the Soviet suppression of the Hungarian Revolution, in the same few days of early November. I understood nothing of the complexity of these events but I listened to the news on the radio and I might have watched some newsreel in the cinema. The ins and outs of the Suez Crisis were far too complicated for a seven-year-old. Anyway, it didn't seem to involve any proper fighting as in the Second World War which loomed so large in boys' imaginings. But the Hungarian uprising seemed very simple. Here were rebels rising against tyranny and fighting in the streets until they were overwhelmed by a brutal invader. Even a seven-year-old could grasp what was happening.

From the next few years I recall Colonel Kassem's revolution in Iraq in 1958 and the Cuban Revolution in 1959, as well as complex and bloody colonial endgames in Cyprus and Kenya. We'd acquired a television by the beginning of 1959 when I made a few entries in the *Eagle Diary* that I'd received among my Christmas presents. My mother insisted on *Panorama* rather than *Wagon Train*. The entry for Monday 12 January records that "I saw what China is like on tv in Panorama." I'd been watching film of gangs of peasants building dams by hand and steel furnaces in their back gardens. I might have seen footage of them banging pots and pans to scare birds until they fell from the sky in exhaustion. This was Mao's Great Leap Forward, in which millions starved to death. I'd begun to take an interest in the war in Algeria. I was starting to watch history unfold. I might have been a partisan for Harold Macmillan in the 1959 General Election, but war and revolution gripped my imagination.

Chapter 6

View From a Hill

Lilburne was an uncompromising firebrand. He had been imprisoned by the bishops in 1638, by the royalists in 1643, by the House of Lords in 1645, and by the House of Commons in 1647. Each confrontation was of his own making, for he had the rare capacity to see a nettle whenever an olive branch was offered him. His charisma was based on a talent for elevating the personal to the universal. If John Lilburne were imprisoned then all Englishmen must be slaves.

(Mark Kishlansky, *A Monarchy Transformed: Britain 1603-1714*, 1996)

Lilburne would end up being imprisoned by the Lord Protector Oliver Cromwell as well.

No-one seems to know precisely, but most accounts concur that John Lilburne was born in Sunderland in 1614 or 1615 of Puritan gentry stock. We know that he spent his childhood in County Durham and was educated at Bishop Auckland and Newcastle Grammar Schools before being apprenticed to a Puritan wool merchant in London around 1630. He fought in Cromwell's cavalry and led the Leveller movement during the 1640s. His older brother Robert was another cavalry officer and one of the MPs who signed the death warrant of Charles I in January 1649. John's thigh-length cavalry boots are on display in Sunderland's Museum. There's a close named after him in Hendon near the South Docks and a street in Southwick north of the river. If Britain had gone Communist then Sunderland might have been renamed in his honour.

The Lilburne boys would have known the coast north and south of Wearmouth and roamed on Tunstall Hills south of the river. The hills would have looked even more prominent then than now. Today they occupy the southern horizon from as far away as Cleadon Hills, and loom ahead as the land rises beyond Ashbrooke south of the town centre. Many times during the late 1950s and early 1960s I roamed these hills like the Lilburne brothers must have done – just as now I follow paths that John Bunyan must have trodden on the way to illegal conventicles in the 1660s until he was thrown into Bedford gaol where he wrote *The Pilgrim's Progress*. From the spring of 1956 I was living at 81 Stannington Grove, half a mile north of the hills we called Tunner.

I'm not sure why my parents moved from Roker to Hill View. They might have needed to retrench financially after my father abandoned efforts to qualify as an accountant. My mother told Vanessa she wanted to escape temptation, in the spirit of *Brief Encounter*, after she'd become attracted to a neighbour. Probably my parents simply wanted to move to part of Sunderland where Vanessa and I would qualify to attend Bede Grammar School, the town's best, if we managed to pass the 11 plus exam that loomed large on the horizons of parents with educational aspirations for their children.

We were the first occupants of a newly-built semi-detached chalet-style house, with dormer windows at the front above a bay window and recessed front door. Today the house is much as it was in 1956, apart from new windows and an enclosed entrance. The front door opened to a hall with stairs on the right. Ahead a door opened to a kitchen and scullery while another on the left led to a sitting room connected by folding doors to a dining room which opened to the kitchen. After a few years my parents added a conservatory where my friends and I would play board games – *Monopoly*, *Cluedo* and *Risk* were favourites – when rain stopped play out of doors.

Sometimes in dreams I'm in this house. Upstairs were three bedrooms around a landing and a separate bathroom and toilet at the top of the stairs. My parents occupied the main bedroom at the front and Vanessa the second at the back, while I occupied a small box room above the front hall. Behind my bed was a raised box accommodating the stair-well. On this box stood shelves for books and plastic model aeroplanes, and from 1963 a Dansette record player and my collection of 45 rpm singles. Above my bed the ceiling sloped downward, with a dormer window on the right. The rest of the room contained just enough space for a wardrobe and a desk plus a rattan cane chair below the window – leaving only a small patch of floor. Here I grew from small boy about to enter Junior School to young man about to sit A Level exams before leaving for university.

Stannington Grove was built during the house-building boom over which Harold Macmillan presided as Minister of Housing in the early 1950s. During Sunderland's peak of prosperity in the late 19th and early 20th centuries the business and professional classes had built three- and four-storied terraces south-west of the town centre in Ashbrooke, along with half-a-dozen grand neo-Gothic churches in which congregations from different denominations would worship. Working men and their families occupied tenements and single- and two-storied terraces near the docks and shipyards lining the Wear, while the lower middle class spread south through Hendon and Grangetown in terraces flanking the railway to Seaham and Hartlepool and roads south and west to Durham and Chester-le-Street. Working people occupied terraces north of the river while middle-class families moved into suburbs by the sea in Roker and Seaburn whence my family had just moved. House-building must have slackened during the economic recession before the First World War. Afterwards the Borough Council took advantage of powers conferred by the Lloyd George Coalition and the 1924 minority Labour Government to begin building council estates in the Ford area, in Grangetown and along the Newcastle Road. Housing Associations built the Garths in the East End, and private contractors built semi-detached houses beyond older built-up areas, for example along the new inner orbital Queen Alexandra Road. After the Second World War the council began building large estates of cottage homes on open fields on the town's southern fringe, mainly to re-house people whose homes by the river and docks had been condemned as slums and demolished. Private developers built estates beyond Ashbrooke's terraces.

Our new home was on the eastern edge of this post-war private housing, separated from a new council estate by Hill View Junior School, built for children from both estates, and an expanse of scrubland which we kids called simply "the Field". The Field would have led directly to Tunstall Hills only a few years earlier, before construction of the outer orbital Leechmere Road from Grangetown to Tunstall Road. Today the Field where we played contains fenced playing fields, but in the 1950s it might have been kept as a buffer between newly-built estates occupied by two big "housing classes" of post-war Britain – middle-class owner-occupiers and working-class council tenants. Only 20 years had passed since owner-occupiers in Cutteslowe in Oxford demanded a wall between their homes and council houses further along the road. In the corner furthest from my home was Hill View Infants' School, which I attended briefly in the summer of 1956. In September I entered Hill View Junior School where I stayed until 1960. Park Lea Road might have offered park and sea-side but Hill View offered a fragment of countryside.

When lecturing on Geopolitics I would tell students about my life-long love affair with maps. As a boy I drew my own version of the map that R L Stevenson drew to amuse his stepson before writing *Treasure Island*. At the Bede, I'd draw meticulous maps in my Geography exercise books. As a civil servant in the Railways Directorate of the Department of Transport in the 1980s, I'd draw the maps needed to illustrate submissions to Ministers on rail closure proposals and electrification schemes, rather than leave the task to junior officials or make photocopies from a railway atlas. As a lecturer I'd enjoy selecting maps for my slides from among the wealth of internet sources. One of my earliest maps, now lost, sought to portray my personal geography – prototype of the map of Hill View at the beginning of this memoir.

I might have been anticipating Jonathan Raban's claim that "[w]e map the city by private boundaries, which are meaningful only to us.... Inside one's private city, one builds a grid of reference points, each enshrining a personal attribution of meaning." Turning left from 81 Stannington Grove I'd pass a police house on the corner of Leighton Road leading to Queen Alexandra Road with the stop from which I could take a bus to town. Across Leighton Road was a corner of wasteland which we called the Bumps, over which we'd ride our bikes. One day Vanessa lost control of hers and fell and broke her arm. Past the Bumps I'd turn left through the school gate into Hill View Juniors and along the path to the asphalt playground. We'd risk injury by walking the tight rope of the top of the gate, all of four or five foot high. Further along the road was a small parade of shops including a chippie and a sweet shop where I'd buy sherbet dips and sweet cigarettes – and then the council estate where I'd rarely venture because of the "rough kids" I'd meet.

Hill View School had been built in the early 1950s in an airy modernist style to serve the housing estates on either side. It consisted of two levels of class-rooms ending in an assembly hall, dining room and the office occupied by the redoubtable headmistress "Ganny" Lawson. She'd cane us for serious offences, while class teachers would use the ruler for minor ones. Hill View had a reputation for getting children through the 11 plus and into the Bede. There were about 120 children in each of four years, grouped in three classes of around 40 or 50. I suspect the classes weren't streamed until the third or fourth year when the children judged likeliest to pass the 11 plus – probably mainly from private homes built since the 1930s – were placed in the top class. Now primary schools are staffed mainly by women. In my last two years I was taught by men. Some of my schoolmates wore callipers on their legs as a result of muscle wasting from polio. I recall receiving the vaccine in a sugar lump administered by a district nurse. Behind the school was a large playing field. We must have begun school around 8.30. My mother would send me on my way after breakfast on buttered and sugared Weetabix and a fried egg and fried bread sandwich. We'd break for play around 11.00.

Most of us would have gone home for lunch around 12.30 and returned around 2.00. We'd have finished school by 4.00. We did what all primary schoolchildren did then. My strongest memory is of building papier mache dinosaurs around a wire frame which we'd paint in lurid colours after they'd dried. Teachers read stories about children among the Displaced Persons after the war as well as the usual child's fare like Frances Hodgson Burnett's *The Secret Garden*.

Opposite the Bumps and school was the Field. In the far right quadrant was a football pitch. The rest grew wild – long grass, nettles, bushes and paths, ideal for play. By a happy chance I was the oldest of about ten children at our end of the street. I had my own readymade gang to boss. My lieutenant was David Parnaby, a year younger than me, living in the house opposite, with a younger brother Philip who served as a foil for jokes. The Parnabys owned a shop selling prams and bikes and toys, though my friends' father worked as an electrician for the NEEB (for which my father also worked). Because of his trade he'd been called up to the Royal Corps of Signals and posted to Malaya before the Japanese invasion. He was captured at Singapore in 1942 and spent the next three and a half years as a prisoner. He was thin, either from birth or maltreatment at Japanese hands. One evening we arrived home to discover that my father had forgotten or lost the keys. David's father must have seen our predicament. He squeezed through the tiny scullery window and opened the door for us. Most importantly David and Philip owned an electric train set which we'd lay out in their bedroom overlooking the Field. We'd transform the rolling stock into armoured trains with cannon and soldiers. We'd set fire to defunct plastic model aeroplanes and launch them from the window.

My second lieutenant was David Kennedy, two years younger and living a few doors away on the same side of the street. Last came two Raymonds, Lindsey and Foley, three or four years younger. A few sisters might be allowed to join our games: Vanessa, and Marjorie Foley and Verity Lindsay. The Lindsays would bring Digger, a companionable black mongrel, to join our fun. We'd play soldiers on the Field – and set fire to what we called "Hitler's houses" comprising sticks and dry grass framed by stones. We'd play cricket across the road using gate posts for wickets. Photographs of Vanessa and me on our new bikes in the street outside our home in 1958 show only one car – a big Rover parked a few doors away. For Halloween we'd hollow out turnips with holes for eyes, nostrils and mouth, lit by stubs of candles inside (which we'd struggle to shield from wind). We'd trundle a stuffed figure in an old pram from house to house soliciting "a penny for the guy". We'd gather wood and household rubbish for a Guy Fawkes Night bonfire on the Field behind the Parnabys' house. After the fireworks were spent and the grownups had gone we kids would place potatoes wrapped in aluminium foil among the embers – only to discard them after we opened the foil and found the potatoes charred on the outside and virtually raw inside. In 1960 I organised our own Olympic Games inspired by what we saw on television from Rome. We would have used garden canes for javelins, hurdles and bars for the high jump, with chalk to mark distances in the long jump. I'd enjoy playing with these friends until I was 13. David Parnaby recalled playing with assegais on the Field, just as I'd recorded in my diary for 1962. He'd gone to Commercial Road Secondary Modern, a former Board School in Hendon. School friends had become more important than the kids round the doors.

At its far end Stannington Grove met Greystoke Avenue, which ran uphill before turning left towards Laurel Grove and Leechmere Road, and Linden Gardens which ran down to Queen Alexandra Road. During the late 1950s the rising ground between these roads and Tunstall Road was being built over with semi-detached houses. Past a big house on the corner of Greystoke Avenue and Lutterworth Road (where in autumn we'd glimpse hung pheasants through the garage window) we'd enter a building site running along Lutterworth Road to the junction with Loughborough Avenue and on to Lambourne Road. From Linden Road we'd enter the grounds of a big Victorian house that had fallen into dereliction. During the early 1960s the grounds were acquired for a Mormon church and the house was converted to the Rosedene pub opened in 1964. As children we'd enter the grounds to climb well-branched trees and catch newts and collect frog spawn and tadpoles from a pond ("the newtie") to take home in jam-jars to makeshift ponds in our gardens. None of the newts survived and no frogs emerged from the tadpoles and spawn. Behind the house was a derelict greenhouse into which we'd venture. We'd treat the building site rising up the hill behind the old house as an informal adventure playground once the workmen had left in summer evenings and at weekends. We'd clamber up and down ladders and run along the planks and swing from scaffolding; or we'd explore beneath the floorboards, free from adult supervision and careless of injury.

I've inherited two school photographs from my Hill View years, one taken in my second year in the spring of 1958 and the other from the end of my final year in 1960. There are 38 children in the first and 49 in the second. All are white. Most exotic were the Benoit twins from Canada, in the back row of the second photograph, with identical haircuts and wearing identical round-necked sweaters. In 1958 I'm standing near the Hitler/Stalin position in the centre of the back row with my upper teeth biting down on my lower lip and the same sly smile as in earlier photographs. I can't identify any of my class-mates. Several boys have a look of Bash Street – "rough kids". In 1960 I'm seated with legs crossed in the front row. I can name most of the boys who'd accompany me to the Bede, and two of the girls – Vanessa's friend Pat Smith (now Burn) from the police house on the corner and Judith Byers, who'd marry one of my two closest friends.

This was Ian Wall, standing at the back with the bigger boys. He's the boy who was so shocked by the freedom with which I addressed my parents when he came to tea a few years later. His father had served in the RAF in the Far East in the war. Now he was working for the leading local estate agency. A few years later he became a partner in the firm and bought a detached house in Roker near to the seafront. In the late 1950s Ian was living in a semi-detached house, slightly bigger than ours, in Greystoke Avenue near Laurel Grove and Leechmere Road – minutes from Tunstall Hill, to which his father dismissed us one September to run off a birthday tea. Ian accompanied me to the Bede where we sat in the same class for five years. After A Levels he qualified as a building surveyor, like his father must have done, but made his career in local government property management rather than in private practice. He's never lost the enthusiasm for revolutionary socialism he acquired in the turbulent early 1970s.

My other close friend was Christopher Pike, sat like me in the front row. He lived at the far end of Stannington Grove. His mother's father, like mine, had been a captain in the merchant navy with a home in South Shields. During the war, never far from our minds as boys, his father formed part of the crew of a 6-inch gun turret on the cruiser HMS Newcastle (sister ship of HMS Belfast moored in the Thames), serving in the Mediterranean and Far East. As a boy Chris dreamt of going to sea. For years he'd read about global shipping in the monthly magazine *Sea Breezes*. Eventually he achieved his ambition, though it didn't turn out in the way he'd imagined. After A levels, he signed up as an apprentice for an oil shipping company. He was assigned to clean out the oil tanks, a thoroughly nasty job which destroyed his enchantment with the sea. After a month or so he decided he'd had enough and went home without leave. When the police called, he hid under the bed. His parents bought him out of his apprenticeship. Thereafter he made a career in banking and rose to be Sales Director of one of the clearing banks. I'm glad to say Chris and Ian continue to thrive.

Our play was heavily gendered. I loved playing soldiers – usually German v. British, though sometimes involving more exotic combinations. I'll have more to say about my obsession with the Second World War in Chapter 8. Vanessa and her friends Pat and Barbara Smith would play at ponies, cantering over jumps on the front lawn of the house occupied by Police Sergeant Smith. In Hill View playground and sometimes in the streets the boys would play Kingie while the girls played Queenie.

For Kingie the boys would form a circle, with legs spread and toes touching, into which one lad would drop a tennis ball. The ball would bounce and roll between the legs of a boy who'd pick it up while the others dispersed. This lad would chase the other boys and throw the ball which they'd try to dodge or punch away. Once a boy had been hit, he'd join the pack who'd already been hit to hunt the remaining boys until only one remained – the victor, Kingie. The boys would form a new circle into which Kingie would drop the ball, and the game would resume. I loved this game.

I'm recalling Queenie entirely from observation. So far as I could see, all but one of the girls would form into line behind one who'd stand with her back to the others. This girl would throw a tennis ball over her shoulder for one of the girls behind her to catch or collect. The girls would form into line again and wait for the thrower to ask if they were ready before turning to face them. The girls would offer one empty hand after another and chant: "Queenie, queenie, who's got the ball? / I haven't got it, it isn't in my pocket / Queenie, queenie, who's got the ball?" The girl who actually had the ball would have to pass it from hand to hand as deftly as possible, while Queenie sought to guess who was holding it. If she guessed correctly, then that girl would become Queenie, and play would resume. If the girl who'd thrown the ball chose incorrectly then she'd have to throw the ball again. I suspect some expostulation might have followed if Queenie had to throw it one too many times. Apparently girls would join in Kingie. I suspect a boy would risk scorn if he joined the girls in Queenie.

When in want of imaginative or intellectual sustenance I'd head for Villette Road library. I'd walk straight ahead down Linden Gardens and across Queen Alexandra Road. I'd walk along Ashbrooke Range and by the grand detached houses and terraces on the right along The Cedars until I reached Ryhope Road heading towards Grangetown and down the coast to Seaham. I'd cross this busy dual carriageway and then walk down Villette Road to the library on the corner with Toward Road leading to the town centre. This library was one of three in Sunderland financed by Andrew Carnegie, the

Bill Gates of the late 19th century, with thousands more throughout Britain, Europe and the United States.

At first I'd turn right into the children's section. At home I had my own small collection of favourite stories by R L Stevenson – *Treasure Island, The Black Arrow* and *Kidnapped* – and tales of King Arthur and Robin Hood, plus a magical compendium of classics like *Alice in Wonderland,* Ruskin's *King of the Golden River* and assorted fairy tales and stories from *The Arabian Nights* (as well as my volume of *Hiawatha).* I borrowed Conan Doyle's adventures *Sir Nigel* and *The White Company* set during the Hundred Years War and his Sherlock Holmes stories as well as adventure stories with a historical or imperial setting by Rider Haggard and G A Henty. I'd borrow the occasional children's history such as a dull account of the Industrial Revolution – which struck me as a tame affair compared with a real revolution, all guillotine and tumbrels, as in France. Later, when I was 11 or 12, I read every one of (Captain) W E Johns' 100-odd Biggles stories that I could find. Sometimes I'd take home several. I can't have been the only boy to puzzle over how a man who'd flown in the Royal Flying Corps (like the real Captain Johns) could still be outwitting Communists and international criminals in the 1950s. In my early teens I began to explore the adult section, looking out for war stories like a bowdlerised edition of *The Cruel Sea* or *Reach for the Sky* about Douglas Bader. For ten years I'd rarely allow a week to pass without visiting Villette Road library. When I visited Sunderland in 2021 I was glad to find the building still in use as a community centre, with the old issuing desk and a small collection of books in the former children's section.

In the other direction, across the Field and beyond Leechmere Road, rose Tunstall Hills – still a magnet for my eyes. My favourite painting in Sunderland's Art Gallery showed the snow-covered hills rising behind a shepherd and his flock standing not far from where we lived. Until only a few years before we arrived there would have been no buildings to obstruct the view. The western hill (now called Green Hill) had a rounded top to which the second presented the rocky face shown in the photograph at the head of this chapter – hence Rocky Hill. By the mid 1950s houses had been built only on the northern side of Leechmere Road backing on to the Field, with a crescent of homes in Myrella Crescent climbing the northern flank of Rocky Hill. In the late 1950s we could ascend the hills from either side of Myrella Crescent by crossing Leechmere Road. The One-Inch to the Mile Ordnance Survey map published in 1961 (but based on 1958 data) shows Tunstall Hills as a rural island about a mile long and half a mile wide, between expanding suburbs to the north and the mining landscape to the south. Now housing encroaches on all sides. The hills seem overgrown and used mainly by dog-walkers.

As a boy I might approach the hills from the east, across the Field and skirting Hill View Infants School before crossing Leechmere Road and climbing the lower slopes of Rocky Hill. Usually I'd approach from the west, avoiding the risk of brushes with "rough kids" from the council estate. I might enter the Field alongside the Foleys' house (next to Parnabys') and continue to Leechmere Road behind Laurel Grove – or I could turn right across the road before continuing up Laurel Grove itself. At first I could walk straight up on to the hills. Later, as houses were built along Leechmere Road, I'd walk towards Tunstall Road before turning to ascend Green Hill alongside a disused quarry. I'd make my way to Rocky Hill along the unmetalled road shown in the photograph. If I were cycling I'd turn into Tunstall Road before making a left turn along this road behind Green Hill. In the 1950s and 1960s there was farmland, and a small farmstead, on the other side of Tunstall Road. People would lift potatoes in the autumn. Now houses cover both sides of Tunstall Road and the quarry is lost among trees. The only way onto the hills from the west is by the unmetalled road from Tunstall Road.

The northern slopes of Green Hill made a fine sledge run, but mainly we'd head for the slightly higher Rocky Hill. By the 1950s the corn fields on the left in the photograph had been replaced by allotments. On the right the road ran for a few hundred yards to a small farmstead where dogs were bred. We could reach the summit of Rocky Hill by paths on either side or by scrambling up the craggy face itself, where we'd find places to perch. On the southern slope of the hills a straggling wood that we called the Dilly ran down towards Tunstall Road and the National Coal Board railway. We'd scare one another about what dark mysteries the Dilly might hide or what foul deeds had been done in a cave beside the track to the kennels. We'd watch steam locomotives hauling clanking trains of coal wagons from Ryhope and Silksworth collieries on route to coal staithes in the South Docks behind Hendon. Eastwards (towards the sea) Rocky Hill sloped gently through fields divided by straggling hedges and laid out for football in winter. Beyond the allotments and the playing fields stood a small farmstead reached by a track from Leechmere Road. In the late 1950s we'd play among bales of hay on the slopes by the farm. Further east was an unmetalled road from Leechmere Road to a second, bigger disused quarry on the southern slope of Rocky Hill overlooking the NCB railway.

As a boy I don't suppose I'd allow more than a week to pass without visiting Tunstall Hills. When visiting my parents in the late 1960s and during the 1970s I'd usually find time for a walk. I took my sons when we visited in 1996. I photographed them standing on the triangulation point on top of Rocky Hill. We looked out on a post-industrial landscape that had changed dramatically since I'd been their age.

The syllabus for O Level Geography in 1964-65 included the economic geography of Britain. My exercise book contains a sketch map of North East England from Northumberland to the Cleveland Hills with notes identifying four main industries: coal, ship-building, iron and steel, and chemicals. The map features boxes opposite the mouths of the Tyne, Wear and Tees, each listing imports and exports. Sunderland's exports are listed as coal, glass, engines, rope, furniture, paper and ships. My notes continue.

> At one time G.B. built ½ the world's ships but in 1957 1/6 and is now surpassed by Japan and Germany. Even so though our exports have dropped it [ship-building] is still one of the main industries using great

quantities of steel. 40% [of ships] built on Tyne, Tees, Wear, 30% on the Clyde, the remainder in Belfast and Liverpool. In the N.E. mainly tankers and "tramps".

Britain reached its peak as a manufacturing nation in the 1950s but was already losing market share well before the precipitous decline in the 1970s and 1980s. Standing on Rocky Hill you can scan the horizon embracing all of Sunderland. As a boy I could look eastwards towards the coast and see the gasometers at Hendon and the cranes lining the South Docks. Scanning past the piers I'd see more cranes along the river banks lined by shipyards. I'd see a cluster of church steeples just south of the town centre in Ashbrooke and behind them the clock towers of the Town Hall and Central Station. Scanning leftwards I'd see the chimney and cooling tower of the power station fed by railway from Hetton collieries south-west of Sunderland. Across the river beyond the power station I'd see the pithead of Wearmouth colliery where the Stadium of Light stands now. Apart from church steeples and clock towers only industrial chimneys and cranes probed the sky, much as in Victorian times. Only in the early 1960s did the first tower blocks join them.

Today the quarry at the south-east end of Rocky Hill is scrubby and overgrown. It overlooks a cycle-way backed by landscaped woodland hiding a school and new housing. You wouldn't guess that sixty years ago it faced a harsh industrial landscape described as evil by a middle-aged man with whom I exchanged a few words as he stopped while walking his dog. Then you might have seen one of the NCB trains clank by. Beyond the railway and the road to Ryhope you'd see a smoking spoil heap, as big as Rocky Hill, fed by a chain of clanking bin travels like the ones in the final scene of Get Carter. Since the 1960s the vista has been transformed, like an Industrial Revolution in reverse. Ryhope colliery closed in 1966 followed by Silksworth in 1971. The power station closed in 1976 and the cooling tower was demolished in 1979. The privately-owned shipyards were amalgamated as part of British Shipbuilders in the late 1970s. The last yard closed in 1988. Wearmouth colliery closed in 1993. Vaux Brewery, the last important manufacturing employer, followed in 1999. My sons and I walked around Roker Park football stadium less than a year before the last match was played in 1997.

One part of this prospect that remains much as it was sixty years ago is the expanse of trees, green in summer and black in winter, in Ashbrooke and the half-dozen church steeples. At the heart of this area is Backhouse Park, fronting upon Ryhope Road and extending south to Queen Alexandra Road in front of the Rosedene pub. It's named after the Quaker bankers who donated their former home Ashburne House and the arboretum that they'd assembled to the Council in the 1930s. After the war the Council rounded off the park with land acquired from the Mounseys, another Quaker family with whom the Backhouses had inter-married. Another section was acquired for sports playing fields. The Backhouses were important members of a local bourgeoisie that endowed the town with parks and public buildings in its industrial heyday. The family sold their bank to Barclays. Ashburne House, the family home, was converted and extended to house the Art College. During the 1980s Chris Pike managed the branch of Barclays that handled the sale of Ian Wall's father's firm to a major Building Society and helped to dismantle other firms that once sustained the town's economy. Ian and Chris have remarked on the steady flight of capital, as well as intellect, which has impoverished the town. Nothing is more telling than the loss of a once-thriving Jewish community.

At some point I encountered the notion – I might have invented it – of an internal map of a town in the shape of a dumbbell. One end represents the area surrounding the home and the other the town centre, with the route between as the bar. I spent most of my Hill View years within a mile or so of Stannington Grove. From the age of 11 the home end of the dumbbell extended westwards along Alexandra Road to Bede Grammar School occupying two three-storied quadrangular buildings (one each for boys and girls) by the Durham Road as it rose from the large roundabout occupied by the Barnes pub. Eastward the home end of the dumbbell extended for about a mile to Grangetown with the Regent cinema where I must have attended a second Saturday morning Kids Club. I have a dim memory of visits with my father by bus and then path to the beach at Hendon, blackened by pit waste from Ryhope Colliery.

At the other end of the dumbbell was the town centre, usually simply "town": the Gaumont, Odeon and Ritz cinemas plus a few fleapits; Woolworths, Maxwells and Josephs for toys and plastic model kits; Chippies behind the station for stamps and models; Hills and Arrowsmiths for books; plus the various department stores – Binns, Joplings, Blacketts and Liverpool House – visited with my mother. The two of us would catch a bus from Alexandra Road opposite the Eye Infirmary. On my own, to save money I'd walk through Backhouse Park, then a few hundred yards along Ryhope Road and finally through Mowbray Park or West Park into town. I might catch the bus home along Toward Road and thence to Alexandra Road via Villette Road and The Cedars; or I'd walk home through Ashbrooke or Backhouse Park. The park was a favourite place. I visited it with my parents and Vanessa as a small boy. Once I awoke screaming from a nightmare provoked by giant cacti in the ornate glass house behind Ashburne House. Later, on a summer day, I might linger on one of the benches in front of the Art College to read a library book or a comic. On hot weekends in summer the family might take a bus from the terminus in Leechmere Road through town to the Cat and Dog Steps. One Saturday in the summer of 1959 I took this bus with Chris Pike and Ian Wall to go fishing in the North Dock. Perhaps we caught a few crabs with our hooks, lines and sinkers. We spent our bus money on sweets and fish and chips and walked home through the town centre and Ashbrooke. At home I joined my mother on the sofa to watch Laurence Olivier as Lord Nelson and Vivien Leigh as Lady Emma Hamilton in *That Hamilton Woman*, Churchill's favourite film, intended to boost morale in the dark days of 1941.

In my first summer in Stannington Grove I endured a few nervous months of bullying by Pat and Barbara Smith's 11-year-old brother Chris. Once he'd disappeared in September 1956 behind the doors of Commercial Road Secondary Modern, I could breathe more easily and settle into Hill View Juniors. By then my mother must have been enduring increasing pain as her spine crumbled. During the winter she was in such pain that she had to spend a week or two in a residential nursing home somewhere behind Tunstall Hills. I dimly recall walking past this building, impossible to trace now, with Dad and Vanessa one gloomy Sunday.

My mother must have wanted to postpone the moment when she'd have to enter hospital for surgery until Vanessa was old enough to enter Hill View Infants School in September 1957. She didn't quite make it. One day in spring I came home from school to find that she wasn't there to greet me as usual. She must have warned me that she was going to have to go to hospital for a big operation, but no warning could lessen the impact of returning home and finding her gone. Vanessa has told me how she accompanied her parents on the way to the bus stop in Alexandra Road. My mother was carrying a small suitcase; she wouldn't need many clothes in hospital. Half way along Leighton Road they halted. My mother must have embraced Vanessa and my father and exchanged a few words. Then she walked on without looking back and turned the corner to catch a bus for Grindon Hospital on the south-west edge of town. My father and Vanessa walked home to wait for me to return from school.

Chapter 7

Let him run Wild

Dreamt about mum. I was living alone in house like 81 Stannington Grove. I went out and when I returned the front door was slightly ajar, as though someone had entered. I went through into the back garden and saw mum with her back to me, hanging clothes on the line. I put my arms around her and woke up.

(Diary, 22 January 2007)

One day in the summer of 1958 I came home from Hill View Junior School and found an unfamiliar woman in the kitchen with my father and Vanessa. She looked stout and matronly, not like the slim youthful mother who'd gone into hospital a year earlier, but she'd have had a hesitant loving smile. "Who's that woman?" I asked. That woman was my mother, home after over a year in hospital for major surgery to correct tuberculosis of the spine.

I don't actually recall this episode even though I'm sure it took place. For 60 years I'd repressed the memory, because it must have been too painful. The only reason I can record the episode is because it stuck in Vanessa's memory. She told me about it one day over lunch after a visit to an exhibition in London. She'd assumed I'd remembered it.

I failed to recognise my mother that day because I hadn't seen her for about a year. I must have visited the hospital once. I didn't lack opportunity: my father took Vanessa to visit regularly but I refused to accompany them. I must have been frightened by the hospital as a place of confinement. I might have felt abandoned. Perhaps I couldn't bear the thought of visiting my mother and having to say goodbye time after time. I might have preferred simply to try to forget about her and just get on with life. I can't say. Maybe all of those reasons apply. How can I know at this distance in time?

Looking back I can see that I would have been adding to my mother's distress, lying on her back for month after month, separated from husband and children. I've had to live with the mystery of why I refused to visit – to endure the impact it must have had on my emotional development. By the time my mother came home I would have had only a memory of what she'd looked like when she went from my life. A year is a long time at any age, and longer for a child than for an adult.

Now I've no way of knowing how my mother felt while separated from her husband and children. My parents corresponded regularly, but Vanessa destroyed their letters when they came into her hands after my father died. She read a little and then decided that she was intruding on their intimate relations and destroyed the letters.

I returned to these events 15 years ago in an effort to understand the reasons for difficulties in romantic relations with women. My marriage of 20 years had ended a few years earlier. My former wife and I had resolved our differences and concluded our divorce. She'd invited me to her fiftieth birthday and I'd accepted. Soon afterwards I fell for an exotic woman whose parents, one a soldier and the other a nurse, had met during the war against the Italians in East Africa. Afterwards they'd run farms in Africa, where my friend was born. The family moved from one colony to another as the empire dissolved. Eventually her father found work with the United Nations Food and Agriculture Organisation. She studied agriculture at university in Britain where she met her Brazilian husband. After 20 years running a farm in Brazil the marriage ended and she fled with her children to a home country she barely knew. I blamed myself for mishandling our relationship after it ended suddenly in humiliating fashion. For a year or two I'd see her occasionally at parties and dances. She described herself on a dating website as a "dressy woman". She stood out in black and red – power colours – the last time I saw her. I'd make sporadic efforts to revive our affair. She'd nourish small hopes and then disappoint them.

The whole business upset me more than the end of my marriage, which I'd seen coming for years. After a couple of years I got over my botched affair. As part of my recovery I sought to discover the reasons for these "difficulties with girls". Just outside Letchworth on the road to Hitchin there's a centre that offered "low cost counselling". For 18 months I had regular sessions with a woman a bit younger than me who'd been widowed and was training as a counsellor. We'd talk about what went wrong in relations with my exotic friend and how to improve my pursuit of love. The obvious post-Freudian place to begin was with my childhood. We didn't take long to alight on the year my mother spent in hospital.

I'm looking at a photograph taken in June 1957, about the time my mother entered hospital. I don't seem as perky as in earlier ones. I lack a tie. My hair's been cut more clumsily. The class teacher in my first annual report from Hill View Juniors described me as "a 'dreamer' who has to be constantly called back to reality. Could do well if only he would concentrate." I had other things to think about. At the head of this chapter I've placed a photograph taken a month later, showing Vanessa and me in a field outside Grindon Hospital, converted from the home of William Doxford who'd founded one of Sunderland's shipbuilding firms. She's holding a posy of flowers and a box of chocolates. She was two months short of 5. I was 8. I can see the faces we'd have as adults. Call us Woeful.

We must have been about to visit our mother. Her lower vertebrae had crumbled. The only recourse was to remove the diseased bone and replace it with healthy bone from her legs. After the operation she'd have to lie in bed for months while the bones knitted. Then she'd have to learn to walk again. You can see how different she'd look on her return in 1958 by comparing photographs taken before and after her spell in hospital. I remember her showing me what looked like a huge rigid corset encasing her abdomen.

My father had to look after two small children. He'd lived in his parents' flat until his late 20s. The RAF provided bed and board during the war. My mother discharged the usual housewifely duties after they bought their first home in 1945. In the 1950s he'd cycle or walk to and from work in the NEEB offices on the corner of Athenaeum Street and Fawcett Street in Sunderland town centre. I expect he'd come home for lunch. My mother would have taken care of the home without the help of domestic appliances like a fridge and washing machine and vacuum cleaner. The Luxdon van would call to collect and return sheets for industrial laundry. Breton fishermen would call with strings of onions over the handle bars of their bicycles. My father could barely cook. Sometimes while my mother was in hospital we'd dine on fish and chips wrapped in newsprint from the local chippie. He continued to work full-time. Big sister Peggie visited for a week or two. Otherwise the only help was from a council carer – Auntie Jenny – who would be waiting for me and Vanessa when we came home from school. She'd make tea before our father returned. I'm not sure how we coped during school holidays. I didn't like Auntie Jenny. She might as well have been Pirate Jenny. She was no substitute for my mother. Vanessa was more tractable. I ran wild.

That August our father took the pair of us for a week's holiday in Whitby. We went by train, in a wood-panelled carriage with pictures above the seats, drawn by a steam locomotive along the Esk Valley. I'm looking at photographs from the holiday. My father had given my hair a severe cut – almost a Mohican. Perhaps he thought it would suit a boy who loved Red Indians. We stayed in a small guest house. When the sun shone Dad would take Vanessa and me to play on the beach. When it was chilly or wet he'd take us on a boat ride or an outing along the coast to Runswick Bay or inland to Goathland. There I had my first taste of moorland. I learned to listen for the call of the Peewit. After supper Dad would put Vanessa to bed and settle down to write to our mother. I'd pick up Rider Haggard's *Nada the Lily*, about a Zulu princess, which I found in the guest house's small library. I'd read *King Solomon's Mines* after encountering Allan Quatermain in my first comic, *The Topper*. That was the kind of tale I liked – adventures from the empire. My generation grew up in the twilight of British power. I recall the last Empire Day in school in 1958. Suddenly, in a few years, it was gone.

A casualty of this holiday was Binkie. My mother must have bought this little brown tabby that I'd enjoy chasing under the bed. I'm looking at a delightful photograph taken in the back garden at Park Lea Road in August 1954. Vanessa, almost 2 years old, squats in the way small children do, looking at Binkie who's just out of view. Aged 5 I'm sitting on the ground behind Vanessa, in a little boy's suit, hair parted, leaning back and supporting myself with my hands. Our mother is on her haunches behind us, smiling, slim and youthful. Binkie appears in two photographs, both from August 1955. In the first she stands in front of Big Gran sat in a chair in the garden while Vanessa stands at her side twirling a large parasol over her shoulder. In the second Vanessa's sitting on the lawn holding Binkie. The little cat had gone when we came home from Whitby. Dad told us she was being looked after. I asked when she'd return. Soon, he said. She never did come back. I forgot about her – but not entirely. Years later Dad told me he'd tried to find someone to look after her, but without success. So he'd taken the family pet to the Vet to be put down.

Photographs from this holiday include one of Vanessa and me at Runswick Bay above the caption "taken after a quarrel!" We're seated on a low wall. I'm sitting upright with pursed lips. Vanessa's slightly hunched, seeming to suck her thumb. Other photographs of us tell a happier tale. The first, taken when Vanessa was two months old, shows her lying in her pram. Her face is barely visible. A hand reaches towards her. The next photograph shows me standing by the pram, facing the camera. The third shows me looking into the pram while Vanessa inclines towards me. Another taken three months later shows me sucking my thumb and looking at Vanessa as she raises her arms from the pram. Others tell the same story. One from 1954, the same year as the first photograph with Binkie, shows me lying on my back while Vanessa sits on me. The following year she's sitting behind me on a tricycle made for two. In 1957 we're sitting side by side in the sun, stripped to the waist, in the back garden at Stannington Grove. Later that year we're holding hands with Dad on the way to the beach at Whitby. The following year, we're enjoying ice-creams on the beach. She's lying on her stomach, looking forward away from the camera. I'm behind her, elbow resting on the small of her back, with an ice cream in hand as I grin at the camera. I've chosen to describe just a few of the photographs. I discern a faint echo of the Walsungs.

When my sons were small they'd ask to hear what they called "naughty Daddy" stories. Most are from this period. I'd recall one incident, from the autumn of 1957 in the weeks before Guy Fawkes Night, when I used a length of drainpipe from a building site as a bazooka to fire a rocket at a passing policeman, and then ran for it. I'm not sure how far the rocket would have flown. I never repeated the trick. Another time, obviously in want of a bicycle, I acquired one somehow and rode it up on to Tunstall Hill. A policeman tracked me down and brought me and the bike back to wherever I'd found it. My parents bought bicycles for the two of us not long after my mother came home, so this second incident must date from before then. I'd recall a third incident from a few years later, when a friend and I set fire to material for a bonfire stacked against a fence near a house. We had second thoughts and alerted the occupants before making a getaway.

The most alarming incident might have resulted in serious spinal injury for one of the gang, Raymond Foley. At the far corner of the Field, behind Leechmere Road where it abutted Hill View Infants School, was a small hillock left behind by builders. Nearby were some discarded lengths of scaffolding pipe. I collected one of these lengths, which must have been unwieldy to handle, and rolled it down the hillock towards the gang perching below. I yelled at them to get out of the way but Raymond moved too slowly and the pipe struck his back. I'm not sure precisely what happened next. One of the gang must have run to tell Raymond's mother who rushed to collect her son. Luckily he escaped with bruising. Mrs Foley called at my home to demand that my father give me a beating. I'm not sure how he replied but he would never lift a hand to me. He would have seen my remorse. Relations with the Foleys never recovered and the family moved away.

Kids in the 1950s were radio kids. During breakfast on Saturday I'd listen to *Children's Favourites* introduced by "Uncle Mac" Derek McCulloch on the Light Programme. My favourites were 'The Laughing Policeman', 'Busy Bee' and 'The Ugly Duckling'. Over lunch the family would listen to a comedy – maybe *Hancock's Half Hour* or *The Clitheroe Kid* or *Educating Archie* (not *The Goon Show* – my mother didn't like it though I picked up "the voices" from friends at school). At teatime we'd sit around a coal fire lit by a gas poker while my mother toasted slices of bread on a long brass fork and my father checked the pools as the football results were read at 5.00 pm. All football matches began at 3.00 pm in those days. Then we'd listen to *In Town Tonight* and afterwards, before bed, to Wilfred Pickles' *Have A Go* – with wife Mabel at the table with prizes for contestants. During lunch on Sunday at 12.00 ("One o'clock in Germany") we'd listen to *Two-way Family Favourites*, from which I'd pick up some of the current pop music hits. Not until early 1958, while my mother was in hospital, did we enter the television age. Soon we replaced coal fires with an electric bar fire and night-store central heating (big aluminium boxes containing bricks heated by electric elements overnight at off-peak rates).

Lita Roza's 'How Much Is That Doggie in the Window?', from 1953 when I was 4, is the first song I recall. Then came Doris Day's 'Que Sera, Sera' in 1955 and 'The Ballad of Davy Crockett' in 1956. I must have been too young to pick up Lonnie Donegan's 'Rock Island Line' when it was released in 1954, but most of the songs I recall from the late 1950s were his – 'Cumberland Gap', 'Puttin' on the Style', 'Tom Dooley', 'Battle of New Orleans', 'Does Your Chewing Gum Lose Its Flavour on the Bed-post Overnight' and finally 'My Old Man's a Dustman' in 1960. Lonnie Donegan formed the musical tastes of the Quarrymen who'd been born during the war and of the children growing up in the late 1950s who'd buy the Beatles' early records. Apart from Lonnie Donegan I liked Tennessee Ernie Ford's rumbling 'Sixteen Tons' and Johnny

Duncan's hurtling 'Last Train to San Fernando' – Nik Cohn's choice as the best British record of the 1950s: "This isn't such a cosmic claim as it sounds. Check the opposition and you'll see that I'm taking no great chances."

My father kept me on a loose rein while my mother was in hospital. As the evenings lengthened in 1958 I'd set off with my pocket money and walk into town, through Backhouse Park or Ashbrooke's terraces, to visit the cinema. If a film was rated A, requiring an adult companion, I'd hang around the ticket office to find a man whom I'd ask to tender my money to buy a ticket: "Please Mister, can you take me in?" I expect I attended the early show, so I'd be able to walk home around 8.00 pm. One favourite was *The Bridge on the River Kwai*. The next day in school I painted the moment when the dynamited bridge disintegrates and plunges the train carrying the British prisoners of war into the river. Another was *A Tale of Two Cities*. I was transfixed by the vengeful *tricoteuse* Madame Defarge. I was moved by the plight of the doomed prisoners in the Conciergerie and by the courage of Sydney Carton as he climbed the steps to the guillotine, sacrificing his life for his friend: "It is a far, far better thing that I do than I have ever done, it is a far, far better rest that I go to than I have ever known." I read the novel and could recite the famous opening sentences: "It was the best of times, it was the worst of times" and so on. Dickens inspired a lasting fascination with the French Revolution.

I might have enjoyed Noddy but I never opened the Famous Five and Secret Seven stories, or the Jennings school stories (I was terrified by the thought of boarding school). I liked William Brown, but I preferred Tom Sawyer. I thought children only had real adventures in the past – like Tom Sawyer, or Jim Hawkins among pirates or David Balfour on the run through the heather with a Jacobite assassin; or, like the boys in Henty's stories, circumnavigating the world with Drake or fighting the French with Clive in India or Wolfe in Quebec. Apart from these history boys, or hunters and explorers like Allan Quartermain, or knights like Sir Nigel and The White Company, or cavalrymen like Brigadier Gerard, only talking beasts like Ratty and Mr Toad had real adventures. I remember how pissed off I was when Ian Wall's father took a bunch of lads on a birthday treat to see *Smiley Down Under*, about a boy on holiday in Australia, when we might have watched Kenneth More exhibit his usual British pluck in *A Night to Remember*.

My first teacher at Hill View Juniors called me "a dreamer" (no doubt bored and inattentive), but I earned an A and came ninth in class. My mother's absence in hospital doesn't seem to have affected my performance in school. At the end of my second year, just before she returned, I came seventh in class, with straight As. My teacher described me as a "keen reader", who'd "settled down", but was still "rather erratic". I was caned on the hand for minor naughtiness and made an occasional visit to Ganny Lawson for sterner chastisement. The father of my class-mate David Oliver was a musician with connections to the BBC. Later David would play in the school group the Atoms and perform at local youth clubs. David's father arranged for us to be recorded for BBC radio. We had to rehearse strenuously. I became bored and disruptive. I was removed from the choir and left to spend my time drawing – which suited me perfectly.

When my mother returned from hospital she wanted to resume our interrupted family life. I was glad to see her but reluctant to lose the freedom I'd enjoyed while she'd been away. My father was never much good at imposing discipline, so the task fell upon my mother. Our biggest confrontations came later, in 1961 when I was 12 and we'd acquired a car, a two-tone (coffee and cream) Hillman Minx with distinctive small rear wings. My mother had taken a part-time job in order to pay for it. She wanted the family to "go for a run" on Saturday afternoons like other families. I wanted to play with friends like I'd always done. I'd make a scene. One day my parents left me behind in a village in Weardale in the rain. Of course they came back to collect me but I'd made my point. Henceforth I was allowed to stay at home. My mother didn't get her family runs. We acquired the car too late, when I was too old and too wilful to enjoy these excursions. My mother never learned to drive. My father, always keen to save money, tried to teach her. One day while performing a three-point turn she reversed onto the pavement and into a hedge, and – after some acrimony – that was the last time she took the wheel. Learning to drive at 17 was a virtual rite of passage in those days. My father taught me well enough to avoid ever causing an accident, though I needed a few professional lessons before I managed to pass the test, after (shall we say) more than one attempt.

I can't recall the precise causes of earlier clashes with my mother but my tactic in the face of attempts at discipline or control was always to run upstairs and take refuge in the toilet. I'd lock the door and open the window and yell "Mummy, mummy, don't hit me" at the top of my voice. What a horrid little boy: I'd have been infuriated if either of my sons had done that. Fortunately they never did, though we had our difficult moments. There were happier moments on Sunday afternoons when I'd join my mother on the sofa in front of the television to watch the Fred Astaire and Ginger Rogers films that she must have seen at the cinema as a girl. My favourite sequence was 'Let's Face the Music and Dance' in *Follow the Fleet*. It seemed to convey something of the spirit in which my parents' generation must have confronted the looming threat of war. Of course I also enjoyed John Ford's cavalry series and other old Westerns shown on Sunday afternoons.

My father tried to engage me in the more manly pursuits he must have enjoyed. After I acquired a bike in 1958 I was happy to cycle round the neighbourhood, but one Saturday my father took me on a long ride to Durham – too far, too tiring. We never did it again. He enjoyed elementary carpentry – especially when he was saving money. We used to have snow in winter. The big freeze of 1963 was just around the corner. The Green Hill was ideal for sledging. Other boys had light, frame sledges. I had one made by my father that consisted basically of three planks of wood – base and sides with a strip of metal along the running edges. It was sluggish to ride and heavy to pull, but cheap. We built the bookshelves for the box in my bedroom, but nothing else. He took me to Roker Park one day but I can't recall the occasion. All I do recall are regular visits on Saturday afternoons to watch amateur rugby at Ashbrooke. I'd climb into the press box with a notebook in which I'd try to record the match as it unfolded. I've never understood the game but I recalled these outings in my eulogy at my father's funeral.

When my mother came home in 1958 Britain stood on the threshold of dramatic change, as described by David Kynaston, our best guide to these years.

> 1959 was the year of consumption; refrigerator sales up from 449,000 (in 1958) to 849,000; washing machine sales up from 876,000 to 1.2 million; vacuum cleaner sales up from 1.1 million to 1.5 million; radio and electrical equipment sales up by 21 per cent; motor-car sales (including exports) up from 1.05 million to 1.19 million; jewellery sales, ladies' underwear sales, money spent on eating out – all up by significant percentages. Even so, there still remained a considerable way to go in the consumer durables revolution: TV sets may have been in roughly two out of three British homes by the summer of 1959, but the ratio for telephones was one in two, for washing machines, one in four and for refrigerators only one in ten.

The numbers were rising fast: a year later 79% of adults owned a television, 40% a washing machine, 31% a car, 22% a telephone and 21% a car. Consumer durables mattered most to women, especially in lower middle-class homes like mine. In the early 1950s my mother used a mangle on a draining board to squeeze water from clothes she'd washed by hand. She relied on Luxdon industrial laundry whose vans would call to collect sheets (each with a name tag sewn into it) to wash and return. She used a carpet sweeper and a dust pan to clean floors. She cut dusters from worn-out clothes. She'd lay coal fires and light them with a gas poker. She'd have to shop daily for food because there was no easy way of keeping it fresh, especially in summer. She was delighted to acquire a washing machine. This was a "twin-tub": she would use big wooden tongs to transfer the hot wet clothes from one tub to spin-dry in the other. Once we acquired a fridge she no longer had to shop daily. She could store frozen peas and ice cream in the freezing compartment, and make iced lollies. All of these labour-saving devices allowed her to think about returning to work, to earn money to buy a car.

My priority was a television. For a few months after my mother entered hospital I'd visit friends (probably the Parnabys) until my father bought a set. I recall *Six-Five Special* ("Over the points, over the points") on Saturday evenings. Once we'd acquired a set my favourites were historical dramas and Westerns. *The Adventures of Robin Hood* was first, followed by *William Tell* (resisting the gross Hermann Gessler, like some kind of Nazi Gauleiter), *Sword of Freedom* set in Renaissance Florence and *Quentin Durward* in Paris in the same period. My favourite was *The Buccaneers* starring the young Robert Shaw (who'd fight to the death with Sean Connery aboard the night train in *From Russia with Love* and hunt the man-eating shark in *Jaws*). I recall a serialisation of Samuel Pepys' Diary with Peter Sallis in the title role and theme music with the refrain: "It's all written down in my diary". Striking a more contemporary note were *The Third Man* (with the zither theme from the film) and the already anachronistic *Assignment Foreign Legion*, which gave me a taste for P C Wren's tales of the Foreign Legion. Westerns were as common as cop shows now: *The Lone Ranger, Wagon Train, Bonanza, Cheyenne, Maverick, Bronco, Gunsmoke* ("Wait for me, Mister Dillon"), *Rawhide* (with the young Clint Eastwood and a stirring theme song), *The Dakotas* (last and best). Have I missed any? Sam Peckinpah's *The Wild Bunch* and Robert Altman's *McCabe and Mrs Miller* are high among my favourite films. No wonder Bert Weedon chose the title 'Apache' for the tune the Shadows took to No. 1 in 1960. Soon I was tuning in to Radio Luxembourg and saving for a transistor radio.

These were the last years in which people took holidays in Britain as a matter of course. I fancied Butlin's, but my parents wanted something more genteel, like the holidays they'd enjoyed in the 1940s – house parties run by the Countrywide Holiday Association (CHA) and Holiday Fellowship (HF) in modest country houses or guest houses in coastal resorts. Our first was in Alnmouth in 1959, then Marske near Redcar in 1960, followed by Aberystwyth in 1961, travelling by car rather than rail for the first time. The programme never varied. We'd arrive on Saturday and on Sunday we'd settle in. On Mondays and Tuesdays and again on Thursdays and Fridays we'd go on organised walks. We'd set off in a hired coach. All walkers would start and finish at the same point, but would divide into groups for walks of different lengths and difficulty. We'd take toilet breaks in a wood: men and boys would go off in one direction and women and girls in another. We'd carry what I regarded as barely edible packed lunches (typically ham sandwiches and an apple or banana) and would end the walks with tea and cakes in a cafe. The coach would be waiting to return us to the guest house in time to change for dinner. Wednesdays were free for the beach or excursions (like the one to Aberaeron). In 1962 we visited Minard in Argyll and Swanage, and Cromer in 1964. Our parents would encourage Vanessa and me to find friends and not hang around them. After dinner there'd be whist drives or country dancing or debates. That's when I would pipe up. I was rather a grown-up little boy.

I was also an anxious boy. I might have begun to wet the bed while my mother was in hospital. I didn't cease until I was about 12. My mother would have been glad to acquire a washing machine. My younger son inherited the condition but received more forbearance from his mother than I'd encountered. She made sure he was able to enjoy sleepovers at friends' houses and camping as I never did. Adults found me a rather reserved boy who didn't take to being cuddled. As the 11 plus loomed I felt a growing burden of expectation. The literary critic John Sutherland described himself as "the family racehorse". I must have felt much the same. My mother wanted me to take elocution lessons and to wear a brace to correct crooked front teeth. I refused and she didn't insist. I still have my "English" teeth.

I recall melodramatically contemplating suicide if I failed the 11 plus. I had no reason to worry. Ganny Lawson described me at the end of my third year in 1959 as "a very intelligent boy – well informed". I'd come ninth in class. Friends would call me, with a note of exasperation, "the walking encyclopaedia" because of my general knowledge. Chris Pike recalled an occasion when I was called to the front of class to answer questions about history. He asked for the dates of the American Civil War. He remembered me saying that the question was too easy and inviting him to choose a more difficult one.

I recall nothing of the 11 plus. My final report from Hill View placed me 11th in a class of 50. Our elderly teacher Mr Duckworth commented on my ability and wide reading but also my inconsistency and nervousness and worry over petty failures. The class must have rehearsed the 11 plus tests, so I'd have been confident when I sat the exam. Oddly enough I do recall a visit to Newcastle with my mother to sit the entrance exam for Newcastle Grammar, a direct grant school regarded as the finest in the North East (Lilburne's old school). I must have been sufficiently confident that I'd passed the 11 plus to flunk this exam deliberately. I didn't want to take the train every day to Newcastle. I wanted to go to the Bede with Wally and Pikey and other friends from Hill View.

Chapter 8

War Lover

And there was Gnotke.

It was a grey November day and Gnotke had a spade in his hand. Eight metres wide, and one and a half deep was the grave that Gnotke, Aslang, Hubbe, Dinger and Gimpf had just finished digging…. They wore no shoulder-titles and no badges and their hands and faces were as filthy as their uniforms….

The last spadeful had been dug. Hubbe and Dinger lifted a stretcher, Gnotke and Gimpf another. Having stuck their spades in the pile of earth and taken up the stretchers, they trotted off and vanished in the mist. It was in the region east of Kletskaya and in the loop of the Don…. Two day's march eastwards lay the Volga and Stalingrad….

And there was Vilshofen

But Vilshofen – that was something more than merely the face and the way of a man. It was the image of a world that was to rise anew out of blood and tears…. It was a march of Might on caterpillar bands, and at the same time one of the hundred fists that were to batter and beat down the will and the independence of other nations….

Vilshofen with his tanks had lain on the northern boundary of Stalingrad.

(Theodor Plievier, *Stalingrad: The Death of an Army*, 1946)

These are the opening passages of Chapters 1 and 2 of the war novel that captured my imagination more than any other. Gnotke belongs to a punishment battalion burial squad; Vilshofen commands a tank division. I bought the novel in late 1960 after watching a film called *Battle Inferno* at the Regent in Grangetown, on the corner of Ryhope Road and Alexandra Road, not long before it closed in June 1961. I might have gone on my own but probably I went with Ian Wall or Chris Pike who both lived only a few minutes away. My mother took the top photograph of the three of us in our back garden before we set off on the half-hour walk to the Bede on our first day in September 1960. I knew about the Russian Front, but regarded it as a sideshow apart from the main action in North Africa, France and Italy. I don't suppose I'd heard of the Battle of Stalingrad, but I certainly wasn't going to miss a film called *Battle Inferno*.

For years I puzzled about this film. Eventually I discovered it was the subtitled version of a recent German film *Dogs, do you want to live forever?* based on a novel whose title derived from Frederick the Great's call to his flagging troops at the Battle of Kolin against the Austrians in 1757. The film had a brutal power absent from British war films. The battle scenes in the frozen ruins of Stalingrad were more vivid than any I'd seen. I couldn't find the original novel in Hills or Arrowsmiths but I bought a paperback edition of Plievier's *Stalingrad*, with a painting of a battered German soldier on the cover. I took it with me when I visited Hill View Juniors to tell my favourite teacher Mr Atkinson how I was getting on at the Bede. I remember his surprise that I was reading a novel apparently beyond my years. Afterwards I could never think about war in the same way. I was awakening to the tragedy of great power politics.

Plievier's an emblematic figure, rebel against the Kaiser's, Hitler's and finally Stalin's Germany. Born in 1892, his father ran the gents' lavatory in the Busch Circus in Berlin. Young Plievier left Berlin in 1909 to pursue his ambition to become a proletarian adventurer and writer – a kind of German Jack London. He spent time as a sailor and knocked around South America, all the while reading widely. He returned to Germany in 1914 in time to be conscripted into the Imperial Navy. He saw action at the Dogger Bank in 1915 and Jutland in 1916 and took part in the Kiel mutiny that precipitated the fall of the Kaiser. He spent the 1920s on the fringes of the radical left before making his reputation in 1930 with *The Kaiser's Coolies*, a novel based on his war experience. When the Nazis took power in 1933 he escaped to Prague and then Paris. From there he was invited in 1934 to attend a Soviet Literary Convention in Moscow. Soon he fell under suspicion of planning to escape to Finland and was sent to the Republic of Volga Germans to help develop "an indigenous culture". By the time he returned to Moscow in 1939 the Great Terror had ended. As the German army closed in on the capital in November 1941 he was evacuated to Tashkent with other exiles.

His fortunes brightened when Johannes Becher, an exiled poet in good standing with the German Communist leaders Walther Ulbricht and Theodor Pieck, found work for him examining letters from captured German soldiers as a way of assessing enemy morale. The volume increased dramatically after the surrender of the Sixth Army at Stalingrad in February 1943 and the capture of over 90,000 prisoners of war. Plievier must have spotted the potential for a novel after he was summoned to Moscow to help prepare propaganda broadcasts into Germany. Becher helped him gain permission from Ulbricht and Pieck to use captured letters and to interview surviving prisoners. In September 1943 he began work on a novel which he completed over the next year. In May 1945 he returned to Germany with the German Communist leaders. He was set up in a comfortable villa and elected to the regional parliament. The novel appeared in serial form in 1945 and was published as a book in 1946. The following year, as the Soviet grip tightened, he fled to Switzerland. He published another two novels in what he regarded as a trilogy – *Moscow* about the German invasion, told from both sides and drawing on his own experience, and *Berlin* about the German defeat in 1945 with a coda about the workers' revolt in 1953. He died in 1955. He was a notable member of the Generation of 1914. His life spanned almost exactly the same years as Captain Jim's.

Plievier shared the same vision of clashing totalitarian regimes as in Vasily Grossman's better-known *Life and Fate.* Grossman's perspective is wider, seeking to encompass an entire epoch, like Tolstoy in *War and Peace.* Plievier's is narrower and more expressionist, resembling Otto Dix's etchings of the Western Front in the First World War. He was able to write *Stalingrad* without compromising his artistic vision by focusing unremittingly on the suffering of ordinary German soldiers, led to their doom by callous politicians and betrayed by cowardly generals, with the Red Army operating almost as an impersonal instrument of destruction.

I sold my original copy of the novel to a classmate in April 1962 but bought a new edition in the 1970s and read it for a third time in the 1990s. Ten years ago I acquired the first English hardback edition published in 1948. Two episodes that have stuck in my memory since 1960 involve a lorry on the way to Pitomnik airfield with a load of wounded soldiers and the desperate scramble to board the last plane as Soviet tanks advance onto the runway. In the first episode the lorry is forced to slow as it enters a snowbound gully. Crowds of wounded soldiers close in upon the lorry, men with "bandaged heads, arms in splints, torsos in plaster, swathed in blankets, rags, canvas, they limped, they stumbled, got up again, and all, even those lying on the ground, all hurried." The driver counts "[t]en grey, crawling, squirming human worms, trying to accomplish what others were still doing with their feet". He accelerates out of the ravine, like "a hunted beast fleeing from primitive men," as "the confused mass of hands and bones on the bonnet, running boards and sides fell off again."

The second episode featured in a dramatisation of a German play based on Plievier's novel and adapted and directed by Rudolph Cartier. It was shown on BBC2 in December 1963 and repeated on BBC1 in May 1964. Cartier was a German Jew born Katscher in Vienna in 1904 who moved in 1929 to Berlin. He learned his trade as a director working for the UFA Babelsberg studio alongside Fritz Lang and Billy Wilder. Like them he left for Hollywood in 1933 (where he changed his name) but found his way to Britain. He was eventually appointed as first head of BBC Television Drama in 1952, to which he brought more than a touch of 1920s German Expressionist cinema. He was the man behind the ground-breaking production of Orwell's *1984* in 1954 and the Quatermass science fiction serials in the late 1950s. His production of *Stalingrad* was part of a Festival drama series featuring modern European plays by the likes of Beckett, Pirandello and Ionesco. It focused on Gnotke and Vilshofen. He portrays the panic at Pitomnik through the visor of a Soviet tank as it advances on the airfield. I missed the first screening on BBC2 as the channel had yet to reach the North East but made sure I watched the repeat in May 1964, although by then my interests had shifted.

My generation grew up in the shadow of the Second World War. I recall a conversation sitting on the front doorstep of the home of David Kennedy, second lieutenant in my little gang. We lamented how much more excitement and fun we'd have had during the war. We weren't entirely wrong. John Boorman's *Hope and Glory* shows the fun to be had by a small boy in suburban London at that time. *Hue and Cry*, released in 1947 and first of the famous Ealing Comedies, shows how kids could enjoy themselves amid the ruins and privation of post-war London. Look out for the small boy mimicking the sounds of bombs and gunfire – just like we did.

My father might have sparked my obsession with war when he took me to see Stanley Kubrick's *Paths of Glory* at the Regent in Grangetown in 1957. Then there were still a dozen or so cinemas in Sunderland. Few survived the next decade. Soon after we acquired our television I noticed a series called *War in the Air* was due to begin on Saturday around 11.00, past my usual bedtime. I stayed awake until then and tiptoed downstairs. I switched on the television and settled down on the sofa to watch the opening episode, full of German newsreel of Stuka dive-bombers screaming down on Poland and France. My father came downstairs and joined me. He wasn't going to make a fuss.

In my first year or two at Hill View Juniors I'd engage in a popular after-school game in which two groups of boys would throw stones and clods of earth at each other. Battle would sway back and forth across Stannington Grove, between the Field and our front garden which I'd use as a redoubt. I'd lead my pals towards the enemy with a bin-lid in my left hand and a stone or clod of earth in my right. When pressed we'd retreat into the front garden. We'd smatter the road with stones and soil. I don't know what my parents thought: my mother was probably in hospital then, and my father at work. Eventually one lad threw a stone that split open someone's head. Ganny Lawson tore a strip off the lot of us in assembly and called a halt.

By the time I encountered *Battle Inferno* and Plievier's *Stalingrad* in 1960 I had a clearer understanding of the war derived from comics, toys, models, television and the press. In the 1950s there was a comic for every taste. I began with *The Topper*. That's where I found Alan Quartermain and his pals. I liked *The Topper* well enough but it wasn't sufficiently improving to suit my mother's taste. During 1957 I started taking *The Eagle*, the most famous comic of the era, launched in 1950 by an Anglican parson to wean British boys from American superheroes, and best known for the cover strip featuring "Dan Dare, Pilot of the Future". I preferred the back-page strip, a cartoon life of Winston Churchill, "The Happy Warrior".

This strip, drawn by Frank Bellamy, prince of British comic-strip artists, told the history of Britain since the 1890s through a biography of its leading politician. I loved the dramatic coloured drawings. I've kept a book containing the complete strip with a few photographs which I bought with money given for Christmas 1957. Inside I kept a later strip – an even more vivid double-page life of Field-Marshall Bernard Montgomery – cut from *The Eagle* in 1962, not long before I stopped taking it. My parents took *The Sunday Times* which featured extracts from Montgomery's *Memoirs* published in 1958 (and Doenitz's in 1959). My father bought the published *Memoirs* through a book club but I didn't get far. It contained too many turgid memoranda and not enough action for my taste. I got more out of a television series presented by Montgomery, and another by one of his generals, Brian Horrocks (played by Edward Fox in *A Bridge Too Far*). In 1961 the BBC broadcast *The Valiant Years*, an American series based on Churchill's memoirs. From 1960 until the early 1970s ITV broadcast a weekly half-hour *All Our Yesterdays* focusing on events 25 years earlier. As the 50th anniversary of the outbreak of the First World War approached there was a big revival of interest, epitomised by *Oh What a Lovely War* staged in 1963. Children growing up then were surrounded by reminders of war – including derelict sites in ports like Sunderland that were bombed heavily.

My first toys, in Harton Rise, were wooden building bricks. From Park Lea Road I remember a big Meccano set for Christmas with which I built an elaborate working crane. By the time we'd moved to Stannington Grove I coveted a double-0 scale electric train set, but my parents decided they weren't going to buy an expensive toy they thought I'd hardly use. Instead they bought a tiny treble-0 scale set that I had to push along the tracks – and soon discarded. I preferred the Parnabys' electric train. My favourite toys, though, were military. Dinky toys took the front rank: Centurion tank, Saracen armoured car, Ferret scout car and – best of all – a 25-pounder field-gun with ammunition trailer and tractor. Dinky also manufactured die-cast jet fighters – Hawker Hunter, Gloster Javelin and De Havilland Vampire, all impeccably British. Last was an English Electric Lightning. The names evoked the fighters of the Second World War. For toy soldiers none could match Britain's Second World War infantry. Timpo's Eighth Army and Foreign Legion soldiers passed muster, but the paint flaked and the plastic was brittle and liable to break. Britain's knights and archers satisfied my interest in medieval warfare. But once you'd manoeuvred the vehicles, and waved the planes, and arrayed the soldiers, all with appropriate noises: what then?

Much more rewarding were plastic model kits. Now they're synonymous with the leading British manufacturer Airfix. They produced their first model aeroplane kit, the Supermarine Spitfire Mk 1, in 1955, not long before I started buying them. This pioneer kit was notoriously crude. It featured only the head and shoulders of the pilot moulded into the fuselage, so that the join between each half bisected his head. There were no wheel-wells for the under-carriage. With aeroplanes you had to take care when applying adhesive to avoid gluing the propeller so that it wouldn't revolve. The trick was so ensure it was loose enough to rotate when you blew lightly upon it. With similar care the undercarriage wheels would revolve.

Other manufacturers were the British Frog and the American Revell. They produced more sophisticated kits (Revell's had sliding canopies) and more recondite subjects (Frog featured the Dewoitine D.520). Between 1957 and 1963 I must have assembled hundreds of kits – not just planes but tanks and warships from both World Wars. I built models of Drake's '*Golden Hind*' and Nelson's '*Victory*', and even a Roman racing chariot inspired by *Ben Hur* which my mother had taken me to see in 1959. She loved a "sword and sandals" epic, especially one with a biblical flavour.

Assembling the kits was just the start. By the time I was ten or eleven I was taking more pleasure in painting them as carefully and accurately as possible. They filled every spare place in my bedroom. One model – of USS *St Paul*, sister-ship of the *Belgrano* which began life in the US Navy – held pride of place on a wooden plinth on top of the television set. Thirty years later, when my sons were the right ages, I recaptured these joys. For a couple of years in the mid 1990s we'd visit the local model shop (long closed) on a Saturday morning to select kits which we'd assemble and paint while sitting around the kitchen table in the afternoon. A few – Westland Whirlwind, Fairey Swordfish, Ilyushin Sturmovik and Aichi Val, all full of character – gather dust on top of a tall IKEA bookshelf in my study, in company with a row of figures from a Gorby Doll which I brought home from the Soviet Union in 1990, ranging from a tiny Lenin via Stalin, Khrushchev and Brezhnev to Gorbachev. Presumably recent visitors to Russia have brought home Putin Dolls – with Ivan the Terrible at its heart.

Finally there were War Picture Library comics. I'm talking about a whole genre embracing not just the original War Picture Library but two spin-offs – Air Ace Picture Library (my favourite) and Battle Picture Library – as well as the rival Combat Library (prose, no pictures) and Combat Picture Library published by Micron, plus DC Thomson's better-known Commando Picture Library, which I dismissed because the drawings were so poor. All were launched between 1959 and 1961. I bought my first in W H Smith's in the south end of the station in February 1960 after seeing *Sink the Bismarck!*

– storm in a bath tub. The market was huge – millions of boys born in the late 1940s and early 1950s with fathers who'd served in the forces. You could have bought a fresh comic every day. Between 1960 and 1962 hundreds passed through my hands. Here are the titles of the ones I was reading in two weeks in March 1962: *Lost Patrol, Dawn Attack, Fires of Hate, The Savage Island, Debt of Honour, Brotherhood of Blood, Cult of Evil, Last Ditch, The Scent of Danger*. Imagine the wry humour of the men devising these titles. I read these comics. I swapped them. With Ian Wall and another lad I ran a little business (we called it a syndicate) hiring them for pennies to other boys. I'd entered the Bede in the second of five forms. I earned promotion to the first form following exams in December, only to be demoted following exams in July 1961. My report contained just one positive comment, from the much-loved veteran Art teacher Jakey Harrison: "Produces very fine drawings". My form master noted my "lack of concentration. I should be happier if he devoted less time and energy to picture comics."

Henceforth I managed to hold my place in the second form, largely because I was able to achieve top marks for scant effort in exams for Divinity, Art and Music, all neglected by most of my class-mates. The only academic subjects in which I excelled were History and Geography, in which I sought to better the highest mark in the top form. High marks in exams for these five subjects enabled me to keep my place. In July 1962 I came 1st in exams and 20th (out of 30) in term, giving an overall position of 8th. A year later I came 6th in exams and 29th (second bottom) in term. No question: I was idle. The form master was not deceived: "His low Term Order suggests he is not making an effort."

By July 1963 my obsession with war comics had faded. Lately I'd been reading them more for the quality of the art work than the stories. One irony is that the finest drawings in this quintessentially British form were done by foreigners. I've discovered that my favourite artist was Hugo Pratt – "the Picasso of comics", an Italian who spent most of his career, apart from a few years in Britain from 1959 to 1964, in Argentina. I'm not going to try to describe the specific qualities of his style, except to say that typically he largely discarded line in favour of block black ink. I'd spend hours copying his work. In July 1963 Jakey paid me the extraordinary compliment of describing me as "A wayward genius". I've hung two examples of my work in my home as reminders that I might have made a career as a strip cartoon artist or book illustrator.

These comics strengthened my engagement in modern history. The usual fare was British derring-do. Some ranged wider. One took as its subject the exploits of a squadron of RAF Hurricanes on the Russian Front in 1942 as the German armies advanced on Stalingrad. The subject of another was a German Panzer regiment's struggle to stem the advance of the Red Army during the last winter of war. One described the Battle of Dien Bien Phu in 1954 and another featured the Battle of Algiers in 1956. I was enthralled by the climax of the war in Algeria in the early 1960s. In 1965 my interest led me to borrow from the library Jean Larteguy's *The Centurions*, about French paratroopers humiliated in Vietnam and seeking revenge in Algeria. A few years ago I re-read it and read for the first time *The Praetorians*, about the paratroopers' role in raising de Gaulle to power in 1958. Apparently they've become cult reading among American and Israeli soldiers training to wage counter-insurgency wars. These are political novels, not action stories.

On rainy days in holidays in the early 1960s I'd sit with David Parnaby and David Kennedy in the small conservatory at the back of our house where we'd vie to conquer the world in our (or at least my) favourite board game *Risk*. I remained unvanquished until the 1990s when my elder son David humbled me (as he did with Chess). I discovered that control of the Americas combined with beachheads in Britain and Japan provided a perfect strategic position from which to frustrate efforts to control the Eurasian landmass, while any player who did manage to master Eurasia would win the game – a sound lesson in geopolitics, evidently not lost on Xi Jinping.

I'd begun to understand international politics. I was primed for our third year History class covering world history between the wars. No other course made more impact. At last I was able to place the Second World War in context. In the following year I was gripped by a course in 19th century British History, prompting a lasting interest in the intricacies of the Irish Question – set to reopen four years later. I'd begun to take an interest in the First World War in the run-up to the 50th anniversary of the outbreak of war. I chose the Gallipoli campaign for a History project and spent three months working on it, drawing campaign maps and sketches of major protagonists like Churchill and Kitchener, Enver and Kemal. I still own paperback editions of Erich Maria Remarque's *All Quiet on the Western Front* and Alan Clark's *The Donkeys* (about British generals in 1915) which I bought in these months. In the autumn of 1964 I borrowed all five of Henry Williamson's novels about the First World War after they'd been recommended in a *Sunday Times* Colour Supplement in August. Williamson was among the witnesses interviewed for the first great BBC documentary series *The Great War*. In January 1965 I read A J P Taylor's illustrated history of the First World War. My obsession with the Second World War had evolved into a lasting passion for modern history.

I've often puzzled about this obsession, which lasted no more than three years, from my final months in Junior School in the spring of 1960 to early in my third year at the Bede in late 1962. I was in no hurry to leave childhood. A photograph taken at our front door on my 13th birthday in January 1962 shows me holding an Airfix version of the FN rifle which the British Army had just adopted. (To be fair, Ian Wall and a newer friend Graham Mole also acquired this popular toy.) In this photograph I'm in shorts. I'm not much taller than Vanessa who's wearing grown-up slacks and resting a hand on my shoulder. My diary (the first since 1959 and kept until August) contains mysterious references to "escapades". These involved capers with some of the old gang such as creeping into the gardens of big houses or lighting a firework behind a neighbour's back door – as well as setting fire to a stack of wood piled against a fence before having second thoughts and alerting the householder. I had no interest in football. Every week from September to Easter I suffered the humiliation of being left among the fatties and swots when the ablest footballers selected their teams. Seven or eight of us would be left to kick a ball around behind the goal at the end of the rugby pitch overlooking the school. A class photograph taken in May 1962 shows me looking much the same as in Junior School. The boys in the front row are all wearing long trousers. Some of the big boys standing behind them are teenage lads, almost young men. I'm among the smallest boys, standing on chairs in the back row. I'm sporting the same urchin's fringe as I'd done for years. I was one of only three or four out of 32 boys still wearing shorts.

I wasn't alone in my interest in war. Ian Wall shared it, until he discovered the fantasies of the supposed Tibetan monk T Lobsang Rampa and embraced Buddhism on the way to revolutionary socialism via standing for Labour in the school's mock election in 1966. Another friend Graham (Paddy) Noble shared my growing interest in the technology of military aviation. We collected books on Second World War aircraft and followed current developments in the weekly *Flight International*. We cut out technical diagrams from *The Eagle*, which I was still reading, and *The Lion* which Graham read. My father took a photograph of us standing beside my mother during a visit to a Battle of Britain show at RAF Middleton St George in 1962. I'm in casual gear including my first long trousers. For years I puzzled over why Graham was wearing his school uniform. Eventually I realised that they must have been his only decent clothes. His family lived in a council house on the southern fringe of town. His father might have been unemployed. Our friendship waned after he won promotion to the top form. Like Ian Wall found Buddhism, Graham found judo (or was it karate?) and free weights.

A couple of years later, studying for O-Levels, I escaped PE and joined Paddy Noble in the weight-training room in the basement of the south side of the quadrangle, looking towards the rugby pitch. We were joined by Adrian Ord (distinguished by the soubriquet Prof, perhaps because he'd mimic word-mangling Stanley Unwin) who'd engage in what he called toe-

up marathons to enlarge his calves. Soon we were joined by David Batty
– Batso, biggest and most thuggish of big boys (albeit a fine all-round
sportsman) – and his smaller, prettier minion David Boyes (Boysie). Batso
transformed the basement into a dungeon by rigging up a selection of
weights into an apparatus for torturing Boysie. In other times and places he
might have found more sinister employment. I feared I'd be next and made
my exit.

As Graham Noble was finding judo (or karate) and free weights and
Ian Wall Buddhism, I was discovering politics. During the 1950s the
world seemed frozen by the Cold War. Europeans still held most of their
empires. The powers were governed by men from the Generation of 1914.
Then around 1960 events gathered pace as the Belgians withdrew from the
Congo, leaving a chaotic vacuum that tempted the US and the Soviet Union
to intervene on opposing sides. In 1961 the US floundered into the Bay of
Pigs debacle in Cuba. East Germany erected the Berlin Wall, and US and
Soviet tanks faced off across Checkpoint Charlie. France entered a bloody
endgame in Algeria. In 1962 the Soviet Union brought the world to the
brink of nuclear war by installing missiles in Cuba. In Britain the Campaign
for Nuclear Disarmament rallied tens of thousands in Trafalgar Square.
Harold Macmillan was winding up the empire after detecting a "wind of
change" blowing through Africa. Juliet Nicolson has identified the icy winter
of 1962-63 as a watershed for the nation, as it was for me. At school I started
attending the junior debating society. In November 1962 the BBC began
screening *That Was The Week That Was* on Saturdays. My parents let me
stay up to watch despite it running until 11.30. I was hooked. I'd watch every
week until it ceased to be broadcast in April 1963. By then the Profumo
Scandal had been unfolding for two or three months. I missed much of the
complexity but I enjoyed the saucy girls and the salacious press speculation
about who'd been having "intercourse" with whom. Times were changing.

My horizons were expanding in other ways. Fridays were becoming film
nights, usually in company with Ian Wall. One evening in December we saw

Sean Connery and Ursula Andress in *Dr No*. For the next few weeks I spent my pocket money on Pan paperback editions of the James Bond novels (and sold them to classmates a few months later). On another evening early in 1963 we were enthralled by John Frankenheimer's *The Manchurian Candidate* which foreshadowed the political murder and paranoia just over the horizon. One Sunday in January 1963 I watched an unknown American sing a few songs on the stairs in a London boarding house in the legendary lost television play *Madhouse on Castle Street*. Later I discovered I'd been watching Bob Dylan on his first visit to Britain. I read my first serious literature – Kafka's *Metamorphosis* and *The Trial* – after the German teacher told us the story of the man who woke one morning to find he'd turned into a huge cockroach. Ian Wall has reminded me that we asked the head of English about Kafka and were disappointed to learn that the author was still on the "to read" list. *Metamorphosis* made the same kind of appeal as Richard Matheson's *I Am Legend* and Edgar Allan Poe's *Tales of Mystery and Imagination*.

By the time winter had turned into spring I'd fallen in love with the Beatles. I missed their appearance at the Empire theatre in February but I did attend a concert starring the Tornadoes who'd enjoyed a huge hit with 'Telstar', and another in March headlined by Gene Vincent, lurching around the stage in black leather dragging a game leg shattered in the car accident that killed Eddie Cochran in 1960. Tony Meehan and Jet Harris (former drummer and bassist in the Shadows) were on the same bill. They'd had a No. 1 hit with another instrumental 'Diamonds'. Meehan was working for Decca as an A&R man. He'd been dismissive about the Beatles when they auditioned for a recording contract in 1962. Times were changing indeed.

Since 1959 we'd taken holidays in Britain. Now, in August 1963, we were about to venture abroad for the first time. Twenty-five years after my mother had visited the South of France we were on our way to St Aygulf, a small resort near St Tropez. The journey took two and half days – as it must have down in 1938. The next time I'd visit France, in 1970, I flew to Marseille in an hour or two. We set off one Sunday in late August and spent the entire day driving to London along the pre-motorway A1 at a steady 30-40 mph that my father liked to hold. We stayed the night in a hotel near Victoria station. At a newsstand I bought a copy of *Private Eye*. The Profumo Scandal had reached its climax: Stephen Ward had taken a fatal drug overdose after former friends and clients failed to give evidence in his defence; Lord Denning would have been working on his report. On Monday morning we took the boat-train to Folkestone and crossed the Channel to Boulogne for the train to the South of France. We skirted Paris in the evening and settled down to sleep in a couchette which we shared with a honeymoon couple (so Vanessa told me). On Tuesday, two days after we'd set off, I woke at dawn and went out into the corridor. I stood at the window as the sun rose while the train rolled south down the Rhone Valley to the Mediterranean. I was entranced – like my mother must have been when she made the same journey a quarter of a century earlier.

Thanks to Mr Google I made a digital visit to St Aygulf. The beach seemed much the same as in photographs taken during our visit and a couple of postcards that my mother mounted in the family album – a narrow strip of sand running for a few hundred yards in front of the small town, with the coastal road on the left and a breakwater shielding a small harbour on the right. Small boats bobbed at anchor by the shore. Not surprisingly after 60 years I found no trace of the holiday village where we stayed. I imagine it was some kind of bargain version of Club Med, with villas for guests and a club house for dining and evening entertainment. I'd read about Club Med in *The Sunday Times* colour supplement and liked what I saw – especially the photograph of a guy with a string of plastic beads in the band of his skimpy black swimming briefs. I thought he looked the epitome of masculine cool: too sexy to carry cash.

Here I discovered the sensual joys of swimming and dancing. I'd done a bit of country-dancing at previous holidays but hadn't been charmed by the music. I'd visited High Street baths for swimming lessons organised by the Bede, but I couldn't get the hang of the waterlogged wooden floats and floundered wretchedly in the chilly water. Now all changed utterly. My diary records that we arrived at 11.00 am on Tuesday and I spent the rest of the day on the beach. After dinner I enjoyed an "open-air dance in the evening" – on the roof of the club house, so Vanessa recalls. The next day I "went in the water 3 times". My diary records that I was "learning to swim a bit". I spent long spells in the calm warm sea, practising strokes I'd failed to master in school swimming lessons. Suddenly I lost my footing among the bobbing boats. I splashed around. All at once I was swimming.

In the second evening I "danced a bit". I did the same every evening. There must have been one or two pretty girls – and probably *une jeune fille* or *ein junge Maedchen* – whom I'd ask to dance. The Twist was still *le dance du jour*. The Beatles didn't hit France until 1964. We would have danced to Chubby Checker's 'The Twist' and 'Let's Twist Again', Sam Cooke's 'Twistin' the Night Away', Dion's 'Runaround Sue' and Chris Montez' 'Let's Dance' – still a favourite in the Art College Soul Cellar in Brighton ten years later. Vanessa distinguished herself by winning the Twist competition. I had to wait until the 1990s before winning my Twist honours in a competition at my elder son's football club social evening. I'll Twist again if the DJ plays 'Runaround Sue' at a dance venue.

By the time we left St Aygulf I'd mastered a rudimentary breast-stroke and lost any reticence about inviting a girl to dance. I bought a bootlace tie which I must have thought was the height of fashion. On the Tuesday after we'd arrived we were on our way home in the night train. On Wednesday we crossed the Channel. On the way from London a lorry drove into the back of the Minx. None of us was injured and we completed our journey by train from Peterborough. On Thursday I was back in school – a few days after the start of term. A couple of weeks later our parents bought a *Dansette* record player for Vanessa and me. I bought all the Beatles' records: 'From Me to You' released in May and 'She Loves You' currently at No 1, plus the first

LP featuring 'Love Me Do', 'Please Please Me' and 'Twist and Shout'. Vanessa bought The Rolling Stones' first single 'Come On', a Chuck Berry cover that peaked at No. 21, after they'd aroused our enthusiasm in July on *Thank Your Lucky Stars*, all in matching dogs-tooth jackets and slim black ties. Her next purchase was the Ronettes' 'Be My Baby'.

Every birthday our mother would marshal the family for photographs outside the front door. On Vanessa's 10th birthday in September 1962 I'm still a small boy, in school uniform with my first long trousers. I'm not much taller than Vanessa and smaller than my mother. At the head of the chapter I've placed the photograph taken on Vanessa's 11th birthday in September 1963. This was the last of these photographs. Little Gran is looking warily at her son-in-law behind the camera. Vanessa smiles to Daddy. My mother beams with pride in her offspring. My father doesn't wait for me to smile. He catches me turning to remark to the females – like a colt whinnying at mares. You can almost smell the testosterone. I'm 14. It's 1963. Sexual intercourse has just been invented.

Chapter 9
Learning the Game

Hearts that are broken and love that's untrue / These go with learning the game / When you love her and she doesn't love you / You're only learning the game.

(Buddy Holly, 'Learning the Game', 1958)

Graham Mole introduced me to Buddy Holly. He owned all his records. Some regard Holly as the master. Bob Dylan would tell how he'd never forget the moment when he made eye contact with Holly at one of his last concerts in January 1959. John Lennon and Paul McCartney revered him and performed many of his songs during the Beatles' musical apprenticeship in Hamburg and Liverpool. Mick Jagger and Keith Richards bonded through a shared love of Buddy Holly as well as rhythm and blues. Keith chose to perform 'Learning the Game' at a concert in Texas in 2007. It was one of the last songs Holly sang to his tape recorder, alone in his New York apartment in December 1958.

Holly had been dead less than five years when I walked into town on the Saturday after Christmas 1963. Sunderland still had the look of a Victorian city, with a few cinemas and modern department stores and some leftover damage from the war. The Central station clock tower and the Town Hall still stood. The wrecking ball had yet to swing. The Beatles topped the charts with 'I Want to Hold Your Hand' and 'She Loves You' at No. 2, four months after being released in August. My parents had bought 'With the Beatles' and 'The Shadows' Greatest Hits' for Christmas. I'd been disappointed by 'I Want to Hold Your Hand' and I preferred the Rolling Stones' propulsive 'I Wanna Be Your Man' to Ringo's rockabilly version. I must have worn my first suit under a short light mac like the one worn by Michael Caine in *The Ipcress File*. I was only a few weeks short of 15. I was on my way to meet a girl for the first time.

Marie was in her third year at Barnes Secondary Modern, across Barnes Park from the Bede where I'd begun my fourth year. She was one of a few Barnes girls that Bede lads would meet after school, to chat or to walk home with them. We would meet outside of Porter's sweetshop at the foot of Durham Road before it ascended towards school, or by the shelter near the entrance to the Park on the other side of the road. Through Facebook I tracked down a photograph from early 1965, showing Marie at the back of a group of younger girls, whom she must have been helping to chaperone on a school trip. I immediately recognised her thick dark wavy hair.

After school on the last day of term we'd arranged to meet at 2.00 outside Hills bookshop in Waterloo Place, near the south entrance to the station and convenient for buses. I can say with confidence that the day was cloudy but bright, with sun breaking through, because I used to record conditions daily in my diary. We took a bus to Seaburn and walked on the sea front. For a time we sat in the Tram Shelter opposite Alex Hastings' shop. I might have summoned the courage to hold her hand. We can't have stayed long, as night would have fallen by 4.00. We caught the bus back into town and made our separate ways home. I lacked the sense to walk her home to Hurstwood Road about half a mile from the town centre, between Chester Road and Durham Road.

I heard nothing for a couple of weeks. Day after day my diary records: "Didn't see Marie". Then on 15 January I discovered – probably from her friend Moira – that she was ill with chickenpox. Moira told me she'd be back in school at the end of January. We eventually met after school on Thursday the 29th when we "talked for about 25 min". On the following Tuesday we went into town together after school and I bought tickets to see the Rolling

Stones (making their second national tour). Did I invite her? I don't know. We met again the following week and she sent me a Valentine card. On the cover are two candles: "Old flames, or not –". Inside it says: "Isn't it time we Went Out?" I must have been slow. The inscription was "To Michael from ? Clue BARNES". After school Moira handed me a note signed with love from Marie. She'd missed me through the hols; she'd been to the baths and on Saturday she'd been in town with Moira. She reminds me we're due to meet outside Hills again, at 2.15 on Saturday 15 February.

I spent most of the morning in bed – as teenage lads tend to do when they get the chance. The weather was overcast when I set off after lunch to meet Marie. The Searchers were at No. 1 with 'Needles and Pins' ("pinza"), the Swinging Blue Jeans at No. 4 with 'Hippy Hippy Shake', followed by Manfred Mann's '5-4-3-2-1', opening music for *Ready Steady Go*. We walked to High Street West to see Charlie Drake as *The Cracksman* at the Picture House – not the most imaginative choice for an outing with a girl, nor the most salubrious venue. Afterwards we went our separate ways (yet again). I watched her walk up High Street. Too late I "realised that I should have walked her home (will she still like me?)".

Not surprisingly she cooled. The next day I record: "Hope to see Marie tomorrow". On Monday: "Didn't see Marie – Why? – she may not like or playing hard to get". Still no sign of her on Tuesday, Wednesday or Thursday, when Vanessa accompanied me to the Odeon see the Rolling Stones ("very good stage act"). They were about to release their first big hit 'Not Fade Away' (a Buddy Holly song from the B-side of 'Oh Boy') which peaked at No. 3 in March. They began the tour as fourth on the bill behind John Leyton (Ian Wall's favourite, with hits 'Johnny Remember Me' and 'Wild Wind', both produced by Joe Meek), Mike Sarne (who had a novelty hit with 'Come Outside' in 1962) and the Swinging Blue Jeans. Among so many artists the Rolling Stones must have played only a handful of songs. I recall 'Route 66', 'Walking the Dog', 'Carol' and 'Not Fade Away'. By the end of the tour they were top of the bill.

Ever-helpful Moira arranged for me to meet Marie after school on Friday. When the day came she handed me a curt note: "I don't think it's fair that I see you any more. I can't come after school and even at the week-ends I go out quite a lot", signed Marie. It was over. Later I added "I loved Marie" to the entry for that fateful Saturday. I continued to play Chuck Berry's 'Memphis Tennessee' (yes, I know the Marie in the song was only six years old). I saw mine a few times during the next couple of years. We went to the same parties and youth club dances. Once or twice I walked her home. We kissed a few times. I kept two short letters from Christmas 1964, one in a startlingly mature hand, when prospects brightened, with Vanessa (at Barnes now, having failed her 11 plus) as go-between instead of Moira. Ultimately, though, prospects faded. The last time I saw Marie, a few years later, was at her wedding reception in the Rosedene. I was learning the game. Within 18 months I'd learned it well enough to spend the night with a girl.

During almost 60 years since these episodes, relations between men and women have changed dramatically, under the impact of successive waves of feminism and big economic change. Millions of jobs once done by men have disappeared, replaced by ones that can be done as well – or better – by women. Millions of women have entered professional occupations that were once almost the exclusive preserve of men. Now young men are much more on the defensive than during the 1960s. Then it was still a man's world, though of course it would have been nothing, nothing without a woman or a girl. We need to remember that the 1960s are as distant from us now as Edwardian times were then. Before the First World War many working men (and all women) lacked the vote. Imprisoned suffragettes on hunger strike were force-fed through tubes passed down their throats. Why judge young people in the 1960s by standards that apply today?

The first girl I pursued wasn't Marie, but Jill (sometimes Gill – I was inconsistent in my spelling), also from Barnes. She was blonde and cool – not dark and vivacious like Marie. I'd returned from St Aygulf with a new determination to meet girls. Some of us Bede boys must have chosen to pursue the girls from Barnes because, in order to evade our attentions, Bede girls were released from school about ten minutes earlier than we were. A few lads from my class must have latched on to Jill and her friends because they hung around near the foot of Durham Road and walked home in the same direction. We sought to accompany them. We might have thought Sec Mod girls a bit more forward, shall we say, than girls from the Bede or the Church High (whence Kate Adie had just departed for Newcastle University).

On 17 October 1963 I record that I "talked to Gill a bit" – first mention of a girl. I'd already fought and won battles with my mother to choose my own clothes and shoes. A few days later I prevailed upon her to buy me a pair of black Chelsea Boots that I must have hoped would impress. I've always loved fancy footwear – Jermyn Street now. On the 29th I invited Gill to join me on Guy Fawkes Night – still a high point in my year, for which I'd accumulate as many penny bangers as I could afford – but she was going to see Gerry and the Pacemakers that evening. 'You'll Never Walk Alone' had just hit No 1. Afterwards I resumed my attentions: "Saw Gillian and walked home with her", I recorded day after day. One day I concluded that I was "getting nowhere, fast", the next that I might be "getting somewhere at last". I was alarmed when Moira's mother saw me waiting for Jill; and another time by my daring to drop the word "virgin" into our conversation: "will she still like me?" (as though she had much of an opinion anyway). Moira mentioned that Ian Wall liked her as well and undertook to find out whom Gill preferred. She told me about Marie and I switched my attentions.

By this time I'd started going to church youth clubs at weekends, largely as a result of encouragement from Peter (Titch) Wilson, from the lowest of five forms into which each of the first five years (to 16) were divided. In 1965 the Bede celebrated the 75th anniversary of its foundation. In April around a thousand masters and pupils assembled along three sides of the quadrangle to be photographed. Unrolling the photograph now I'm struck most of all by the absence of a single non-white face. I'm in the back row just right of centre, jacket open, hair brushed to one side, and scowling. I was pissed off about having to stand on a bench for an unconscionable time. Titch stands 12th from the left in the second row from the back. By then our friendship had cooled. Reflecting on the past year in my diary for 1964 I dismissed him brutally: "Getting sick of Wilson." I'd found other friends and seemed to be "[d]oing quite well at close of year with girls."

Titch was the kind of working-class Grammar School boy whom Brian Jackson and Dennis Marsden describe in their classic *Education and the Working Class* (1962) as drifting into the lower forms as a result of increasing disaffection with school, especially as the rival attraction of girls began to be felt. He lived in a terrace near the town centre, not far from Graham Mole. I mention him in my diary for the first time in May 1962. By 1963 he'd become a companion on visits to the cinema. That autumn he persuaded me to attend St Nicholas' Youth Club near the junction of Alexandra Road and Durham Road before it ascended to the Bede. Don't under-estimate the significance of this decision. Later I tried to persuade my friend Bruce Cummings to accompany me. Bruce lived nearby. We'd walk to and from school. But he declined, so our friendship cooled. In March 1964 Titch and I went to see *The Great Escape*. One Saturday in May he visited my home and we walked into town, probably to spend time with records in Atkinsons. On a similar outing in June we were joined by a newer friend Graham Mole, but Titch was my companion at St Nich's in the evening. He left school without a single O Level. The last time I saw him was among the faces in the Bis Bar on Park Lane in early January 1966. A month later I heard on *Police Call* that he'd run away from home. In early 1968 I record that he'd lost an eye in a car accident. Through Facebook I discovered that he'd died years ago. Some are born unto trouble. I recall him as the friend who encouraged me to get out on a weekend evening – which in 1963 aged 14 meant visiting church youth clubs.

Church youth clubs seem to have been overlooked in accounts of the 1960s. For three years, between late 1963 and 1966 when I was 17, they were at the centre of my social life, as for my friends. They brought together the mid-teen boys and girls in an area based on age rather than school or work. They catered for youngsters who were still at school, with only pocket money to spend, and the majority who'd left school and started earning but were still too young to be served readily in pubs. We tend to forget that most youngsters left school at 15 for jobs that required few if any formal qualifications. About 150 boys (in five classes) entered the Bede in 1960. 140 obtained at least one O Level in 1965 (so Titch was unusual in obtaining none). Seventy entered the Sixth form but only around 20 qualified for a "major award" in the form of a state scholarship for university (though others received local authority support or went into other forms of higher or further education). Bede girls tended (like Ian Wall's girl-friend Judith Byers) to go to teacher-training colleges rather than university.

When I began attending St Nich's, where I'd attended Sunday School just a few years previously, we'd play table tennis and dance to records. There was no alcohol but a lot of smoking. My parents had stopped as a result of publicity about lung cancer and I never started. On Friday 29 November 1963 I was walking home from St Nich's along Alexandra Road with friends when someone told us that President Kennedy had been shot. By then the British Beat Boom was well under way. Don Airey from the year above me at school and David Oliver from my year formed the Atoms who'd play at St Nich's and at concerts and dances at school in 1964. Listen to the Rolling Stones' first LP, released in April, and you'll get an idea of what they'd perform – covers of Chuck Berry and Bo Diddley, Muddy Waters or Howlin' Wolf, and compelling versions of Leadbelly's 'John Henry' and 'Tell Me', the sole Jagger-Richards song on that first LP. Pat Smith tells me that the Green Onions were the equivalent group from Southmoor Technical School, who'd play at their dances. The Fireflies and the Jazz Board, both led by Nigel Olsson, played at St Nich's before he left for London as part of Plastic Penny with Mick Grabham, brother of one of Vanessa's friends. Don Airey played piano in the Atoms. Since the 1970s he's played keyboards in most British heavy metal bands. Olsson began drumming for Elton John in 1969. They performed at the Stadium of Light while I was making final revisions. Olsson's described himself as a "descriptive drummer" who plays to the lyrics and the piano – as you can see (and hear) in a YouTube video which shows him in action on 'Saturday Night's Alright for Fighting' in concert in 2012. There were other youth clubs but St Nich's was the place for live music.

I soon recovered from the debacle with Marie. One Friday evening in May at Christ Church youth club I summoned the courage to kiss all of three girls on the lips – no doubt just light pecks – and sought unsuccessfully to walk one of them home. For a week or two in June I'd meet another girl from Barnes school at lunchtime in Barnes Park, where we'd chat and hold hands. I took her to see Ken Russell's *French Dressing* (then an oddity and now a minor classic) and put my arm round her (further than I'd ventured with Marie); but she lived too far away to walk home, and a friend told me that she wasn't going to meet in the park again. I had Graham Noble as my companion for *Zulu* and Vanessa for *A Hard Day's Night* (as earlier for *Summer Holiday*).

I've described the impact of my week in St Aygulf in 1963. We love holidays precisely for the opportunity for adventure and personal transformation. In August 1964 we went back to CHA, spending two weeks in Cromer in the same guest house – Abbeville, in Cabbell Road above the promenade west of the pier – in which my parents stayed in 1948. I own three photographs from that year. First is a class photograph taken in May. I'm in almost exactly the same position as in the equivalent one from 1962 – the Hitler/Stalin spot in the back row. I'm looking into the camera with a self-possessed air. The urchin's grin has gone. My hair's longer and neatly parted. Second is a group photograph taken at the front door of Abbeville. I'm at the back, beside two other youths, tall and serious. Last were the ones taken at my father's family gathering in Lowestoft, in which I'm looking slightly detached, as though embarrassed by the occasion. I'm almost grown.

Mr Google reassures me that Abbeville survives, albeit dowdier than in the 1960s. The rear still opens onto Evington Gardens where I enjoyed my first proper snog on Sunday after we arrived: "Necked with Penny for about 15 mins in evening. Put my tongue inside her mouth touching her tongue – luscious!! Touched her right breast lightly – no objection – kissed about 10-12 times." Necking – we all used the term, and petting, current since at least the 1920s (you can find it in Scott Fitzgerald's *This Side of Paradise* and Aldous Huxley's *Point Counter Point*). On Monday there was more necking in the coach returning from the usual excursion, and again on Tuesday. Now I'd had my turn. Penny told me that she wanted a "mad time". On Friday another lad told me he'd been to bed with her: "his hands went everywhere. I don't think they made love – she was too intelligent to do that for it could ruin her life." I'd been impressed when she told me she was "[T]op of her year at school."

I had no idea about contraception and I don't suppose she did. The pill didn't become available for single women until around 1970. "Illegitimate" babies, still called "bastards", were a standard trope for novels like Stan Barstow's *A Kind of Loving* (1960) and Margaret Drabble's *The Millstone* (1963) and for films like *A Taste of Honey* (1961) as well as on television and in the press. Single mothers would face stigma and pressure to give up their babies for adoption; or the prospective parents would "have to get married", like Prof Ord did soon after leaving school in 1965, the same year in which Roy C had a hit with 'Shotgun Wedding'. Anyway, by Friday I'd latched on to Judy, a plain girl who grumbled about her adoptive parents. We exchanged a few kisses. Penny and Judy left on Saturday and no new girls arrived. I read a silly pulp novel (spin-off from a film starring Oliver Reed and David Hemmings) called *The System* about lads on the pull. When there wasn't an excursion I went girl-watching on the beach. Of an evening I'd wander the amusement arcades and pier. I met a girl staying in a guest house opposite Abbeville: "held her hand, arm round waist, and kissed about 6 or 7 times". On the last evening I got a little "happy" on cider at a party back in Abbeville.

Once again I was full of confidence when I returned to school in September. "Might try to get off with Jill again," I resolved, "dying to kiss and hold a girl again." Jill (I used G and J indifferently), aged 14, would have started her final year. She too would have matured since our early encounters. She gave me short shrift: "saw Jill, and, because of Brick [Ian Wall] and against my better judgement, I asked her 'if she was doing anything tonight' – 'Yes' – 'Sure' 'Yes'. If at first you don't succeed, try, try again." I missed her the following day. One of Batso's cronies told me: "Jill didn't like me – well at least now I know". I looked elsewhere, patrolling the town centre: "Met a girl down town but Batty came along and picked her up – Blast!" Afterwards I met Graham Mole and we resumed our prowl. And so, presumably, it must have gone, as that's the last regular entry.

Guy Fawkes Night had long been one of the big nights of my year. After the last banger had been thrown and the bonfires had subsided I was hanging around the field beside Barnes Park with four other lads, including Ian Wall and Alan Pullan, not one of my usual cronies, when we met a couple of girls. Soon Pullan paired off with Pat and I did with Judith. All I remember of Judith is that she was a slender girl with long dark hair and wore stockings and suspenders. Maybe Pat was blonde. The girls were 14. Pullan and I were 15. The four of us went into Barnes Park where we found secluded spots behind bushes by the lake. I'll forbear to quote the detailed narrative, running from Thursday's entry until Saturday's in my *School-boy's* diary. Suffice to say that Judith did "[l]icence my roving hands, and let them goe / Behind, before, above, between, below." She'd become "my America, my new found lande." I came home with a small bite on my lip and the scent of "sap that smells strange on [my] fingers".

My parents and Vanessa would be out on Tuesday evening, so I invited Pullan and the girls to my home where we spent a couple of hours in the living room enjoying the same kind of fun as on Guy Fawkes Night. A week after our first encounter I put on my favourite short white mac (no dark brown overcoat) and walked over to Judith's home in Thorney Close a couple of miles away. We took a stroll along an unlit lane and lay among dry leaves to enjoy more "necking and petting". I visited her home again the next evening (Friday) but made an early departure when an unexpected boyfriend arrived. We arranged to meet on Monday but I must have decided things were getting complicated: "Finished with Judith – hearty sigh of relief – hooray." When I ran into her in January I described her as a "horrible thing – she's best forgotten though I enjoyed her at the time". A few days later I complained to my diary that Pullan was "going on about that awful ___ – she was just a pros – I should have had nothing to do with her". Like youths since as far back as the 1920s we talked about "birds" and distinguished between the fast and the loose – as they were still doing in the 1970s if Nick Hornby can be believed. The next time I saw Judith was in 1970, at the bus-stop outside the Alexandra pub in Grangetown. She had a man and two kids with her. She'd have been 20.

I've often wondered why I began pursuing girls with such vigour at such a young age. My father failed to inspire me with his life-long enthusiasm for sport – though we watched Cassius Clay's bouts with Sonny Liston and Henry Cooper on television. Dad loved boxing. His hero was Rocky Marciano, world heavyweight champion from 1952 until 1956, when he retired undefeated. When school friends would spend Saturday afternoons at Roker Park watching Sunderland, I'd have been assembling and painting plastic models. I visited Roker Park once, in March 1965, when Sunderland beat Notts Forest 4:0 (as I noted in my diary). I wasn't inspired to go again. By 1963 I'd put Biggles and war comics behind me. That summer I read Mika Waltari's novel *The Egyptian* about the heretic pharaoh Akhnaten. I went on to read every book on Ancient History that I could find in Villette Road Library. On dull days during the summer holidays in 1964 I'd visit the Central Library to read *War and Peace*. I'd been enchanted by Audrey Hepburn as Natasha in King Vidor's 1956 film, which I'd seen at the Theatre Royal in Bedford Street which specialised in revivals. In the novel I got bogged down at Borodino. I would be reading when other boys were watching or playing football. I took no part in the sporting life of the school. I had time and attention to spare for girls.

I resembled my mother. Like her, I was the senior sibling. My father put no pressure upon me whereas I'd been conscious of carrying the burden of her expectations since the 11 plus. Like my mother I enjoyed dancing. We'd watched Fred and Ginger together on Sunday afternoons. I savour the moment when I enter a dance venue in white linen shirt and black chinos and black dress shoes. When I came home on a Monday evening in the mid 1960s I'd find my mother in front of the television watching *Come Dancing*. I was never one of those lads who'd stand by the wall while the girls danced around their handbags. If I liked a record I'd ask one to dance. If she declined I'd ask another. I'd grown up surrounded by forceful females who fussed over me. I had a companionable sister with older friends whom, like Pat Smith, I often knew. I understood what was happening in the lives of teenage girls. I'd have known better than many boys how to talk to them. By the time I was 15 I'd grown into a personable lad, albeit lacking the appeal of the big sporty lads and the musicians. What Pullan and I had in common on Guy Fawkes Night in 1964 was that we understood and liked women and girls: he'd coo the Supremes' 'Baby Love', which was climbing towards No. 1 in November 1964, and would spend lunchtimes at a Bingo club in the town centre.

I'd felt the first quickening of sexual interest in my final year at Hill View. I noticed the budding breasts of the bigger girls. I made smutty drawings to amuse a girl sitting at the desk beside mine. In my second year at the Bede I paid a few pence to borrow Batso's brown paper-covered copy of *Lady Chatterley's Lover*. It fell open at what we called the dirty bits. I bought Simone de Beauvoir's *Brigitte Bardot and the Lolita Syndrome* for Richard Avedon's photographs of the sexy lady. In January 1963 I went to see *Gypsy* because it was about a striptease dancer – and also because I'd enjoyed glimpses of Rosalind Russell singing 'Everything's coming up roses', and Natalie Wood entertaining the punters, in a trailer I'd seen the previous week. A few days later I "[b]ought Nude Book" (probably *Health and Efficiency*, with black-and-white airbrushed photographs of ordinary naked women) in a newsagent in Silksworth Row round the corner from the swimming baths. I paid 2/6 and sold it to a classmate for 3/6. I educated myself from a book called *The Opposite Sex* which I bought from the paperback stall in Jackie White's Market and rented to curious classmates. At home around the television we made jokes about Rudolf Nureyev's bulge and buttocks. We'd talk freely around the dinner table – to the surprise of Ian Wall when he came to tea one Saturday early in 1963. A year later I told him that Baden-Powell had spouted "rubbish" in *Scouting for Boys* when warning about masturbation leading to madness. My mother seemed untroubled when she found a tatty paperback *Lolita* in my school rucksack. She indulged me when I bought a pack of naughty French playing cards featuring scantily-clad and naked women as a souvenir from St Aygulf. Vanessa and I grew up without shame or embarrassment about our bodies. She'd tease me about my liking for what are now called budgie smugglers. She bounced into my bedroom one morning to tell me that she'd begun menstruating. In communal showers after games I'd check other lads' sprouting pubic hair against my own growth. Periodically I'd measure my growing parts and record the results in my diary.

My other passion was pop music. In other times the stars of the 1960s might have pursued careers as novelists, script-writers, painters, actors or directors. Then they chose popular music. You had to grow up in those years to appreciate how extraordinarily rapidly pop music developed. In 1963 the Beatles took Britain by storm, followed by other Liverpudlian groups like Gerry and the Pacemakers, Billy J Kramer and the Dakotas, the Searchers, the Merseybeats, the Fourmost and the Swinging Blue Jeans, recording Lennon-McCartney or covers of American records. In 1964 the Beatles conquered the West. The Rolling Stones broke through, followed by the Kinks, Manfred Mann and the Animals. I saw the Stones at the Odeon again in 1965, just after they'd released 'The Last Time', their first No. 1 hit composed by Jagger-Richards – albeit borrowed from the Staple Singers' version of a traditional song. The Who broke through in 1965. By then the Americans had launched their counter-offensive, spear-headed by the Beach Boys. Black music had begun to cut through, first with the Supremes in 1964 and then followed in 1965 by other Motown stars (a review toured Britain that year) and by Otis Redding and Wilson Pickett on Ahmed Ertegun's Atlantic label. In March 1966 I watched James Brown perform live on *Ready Steady Go* – "great", I told my diary. By then Bob Dylan had found the electric guitar and the Byrds had invented Folk-Rock. The Lovin' Spoonful, Mamas and Papas, and Simon and Garfunkel had hits in Britain in 1966. The Beach Boys released *Pet Sounds* and the Velvet Underground and Nico began performing as part of Andy Warhol's Exploding Plastic Inevitable. Jac Holzman signed the Doors to Elektra and Grace Slick started singing with Jefferson Airplane. Jimi Hendrix and Cream hit the charts in Britain. Pink Floyd began playing in London clubs.

I loved the Beatles' 'Please Please Me' when it came out in the bleak late winter of 1963. In June, after they'd released 'From Me to You', I'd rush home from school on Tuesday to listen to *Pop Go The Beatles* at 4.30 on the Light Programme. By 1964 I'd transferred my allegiance to the Stones, Manfred Mann and the Animals. I'd watch *Top of the Pops* on Thursdays and take the bus into town at lunch-time on Friday to spend my pocket money on an outstanding new record, like the Animals' 'House of the Rising Sun', the Moody Blues' 'Go Now', the Righteous Brothers' 'You've Lost that Lovin' Feeling' or Them's 'Baby Please Don't Go' (with 'Gloria' on the B-side). I acquired a musical education from teenage Norman Jopling's articles in *Record Mirror* about "great unknowns" among American R&B singers. In late 1963 I picked up Marvin Gaye's 'Can I Get a Witness' and Martha and the Vandellas' 'Heatwave' on Radio Luxembourg, like signals from a distant planet. On Saturday mornings I'd call at Graham Mole's home in Elmwood Road behind the Royal Infirmary and we'd set off on a tour of grimy junk shops in Chester Road, Hylton Road and High Street East in search of obscure American records and hits from the late 1950s and early

1960s. Sometimes Ian Wall would join us. We'd go back to Graham's home to play and swap our acquisitions. On my own I'd rifle through discounted records in Atkinsons in Athenaeum Street or White's Market. I was a terrible music snob. I bought the Kingsmen's 'Louie Louie' and sneered at the Kinks' cover. I brought the Jaynetts' 'Sally Go Round the Roses' to play in our Music class. It might not have impressed my classmates but it inspired John Cale and Lou Reed as they assembled the Velvet Underground. I was primed for Bob Dylan's 'Subterranean Homesick Blues' and the Byrds' 'Mr Tambourine Man', blown away by their effortless cool when they performed on *RSG* in August 1965.

The 1960s were a golden age of comedy as well as music. We'd recite morsels from 'The Blood Donor' and 'The Radio Ham'. Some acquired a taste for satire from *That Was The Week That Was*. Most of all in the mid 1960s we relished the dialogues between Peter Cook and Dudley More – the Lennon and McCartney of comedy – in *Not Only But Also*. Don Airey was not only a fine journeyman musician but also a skilful improviser when he and Dick Temple channelled Pete and Dud in school concerts in 1965. I found them funnier than the originals; you had to be there. I devised a couple of sketches, one about Stanley and Livingstone and another in which a few lads with arms by their sides and footballs between their ankles jostled like Emperor Penguins incubating eggs. Feeble, I know, but we're talking schoolboy humour. One concert came to an abrupt end when a few lads at the front of the hall started throwing pennies on to the stage during a trumpet solo by one of the masters. They paid a visit to the headmaster's study to have their trouser seats warmed.

After Judith the girls are just names in the diary. On the Saturday evening after I'd run into her unexpected boyfriend I met June – "nicer than the girl Judith" – at the weekly dance at St Nich's. We'd meet there for a few weeks. I took her to see John Huston's film of Tennessee Williams' *Night of the Iguana* featuring Richard Burton and Ava Gardner. I didn't make much sense of it and I don't suppose she did. Soon I'd dropped June and by Christmas

I'd found Jacqueline. We went to a New Year's Eve party and then to see *Carry On Cleo*: "quite good – very funny – some really 'blue' jokes (about eunuchs)". Soon I broke with her: she was a bit plump (never a good look) and I had revived hopes of Marie. She was followed by Felicity (miscalled Facility), Anne and Susan – mere names in my little red book (though I recall a kiss from Felicity at the back door to a grand house overlooking Ashbrooke rugby ground). What I was seeking was a girl as sexually accommodating as Judith but smarter in both senses of the word. In April I resolved to concentrate on my approaching O Levels: "No more sex for me till after the G.C.E."

I'd been monitoring test and exam marks in my diary since January 1962 but by 1964 I'd begun to mature intellectually – perhaps because what we were studying ceased to be quite so mechanical (in Jackson and Marsden's term) and offered more scope for expression, as with my History project on Gallipoli. When I cleared the garage I found a record of reading that the English teacher, Plob Smith, encouraged us to start keeping. Entries for 1964 (aged 15) included *Metamorphosis* and *The Trial* as well as popular rubbish like Dennis Wheatley's *The Devil Rides Out* and T Lobsang Rampa's *The Third Eye*. In the common room at Cromer one evening I picked up the Penguin edition of E M Forster's short stories and read 'The Machine Stops', written before the First World War but anticipating today's digital world more accurately than better-known dystopian novels. That autumn I read Williamson's war novels and Robert Graves' *I Claudius* and *Claudius the God*. During the Christmas holidays I was reading A J P Taylor's *First World War* ("very good though more like an essay") and continuing into 1965 with *Lord of the Flies*, *The Time Machine*, *For Whom the Bells Tolls* and Sholokhov's *Virgin Soil Upturned* (about Soviet collectivisation). I would have scorned the condescension of "young adult fiction" if the category had existed.

At last in the Fifth form, in the run-up to O Level GCEs, we were getting the chance to write essays on substantial topics. In October I wrote what the English master rated as an "eminently rational & well written" response to the very 'Sixties' question he'd set: "Are too many restrictions imposed by adults upon people of our age?" I suggested votes at 18. In another, on ways of improving the town centre, I called for the replacement of grimy old buildings (not imagining the demolition of the Town Hall within a few years). In December, while I was looking forward to Christmas parties and hoping to meet Marie, I used the set topic of 'Discontent' to offer a synoptic view of history and politics.

> Discontent has been one of the great motive forces of mankind throughout History. It has been at the root of all of the great revolutions.... It is now the cause of the continual turmoil of the underdeveloped countries of Africa and Asia. Discontent, however, never grows of its own accord; at its roots are the various sufferings that have plagued mankind from time immemorial; famine, poverty, autocracy, persecution being only four out of many.

> The discontent of nations can only be effective when organised by men of exceptional ability. These men have been able to harness the dissatisfaction of nations to further their own ambitions. This has been a relatively common occurence [sic] in the last half-century and has been caused mainly by the weakening effect of the First World War on its participants and the inability of the more backward countries to readjust themselves to the modern world.

> In these countries the social system was, in countries like Russia, China and the Austro-Hungarian Empire, autocratic with a very large class of landless peasants thus giving rise to discontent. These countries fell prey to the revolutionary idealists such as Lenin and Mao Tse-tung who used this discontent to seize power and set up dictatorships. The Chinese are now encouraging this type of movement in the ex-colonial countries of Africa, wishing to substitute communism for imperialism.

The essay goes on to acknowledge working-class grievances in the 19th century while deprecating current disputes in tones that I'd picked up from my parents around the dinner table. It concludes by reflecting that "though discontent has been evident in most revolutions whether it erupts in violence is dependent on the social structure of the country, its achievements abroad and the temperament of the people." The essay earned a high mark and the comment "extremely well written". I devoted more attention than to any previous effort. An exercise book for rough work contains a draft of the entire essay and a revised introduction. I wasn't just chasing girls and collecting obscure American records.

As O Levels (often called the school leaving exam) approached I had to start thinking about life beyond school. My performance had reached a low point in July 1963 when I was placed second from bottom in Term order and saved my position in class only by coming 6th in exams. I'd gained ground by December but headmaster Mr Budge insisted that I "must make a more serious effort in [my] weaker subjects". I had no idea what to do after leaving school, apart from vague thoughts of Art College which my parents did nothing to encourage. My diary records that I attended a "carriers [sic] exhibition" in May 1964, but I found no inspiration. My main interests were girls and music. My closest friend was still Titch Wilson, in the bottom class and destined to leave school without any qualification. I improved my position in the July exams but was warned once again that I had "too many weak subjects" and would have to "make a real effort for G.C.E. year".

I've always been as fascinated by the Bolsheviks as by the Jacobins. As the year began I conducted myself like any Bolshevik would do. I began to storm – to work intensively. I had three weak subjects – French, Physics and Maths. For French I sat beside an even weaker linguist whom I sought to coach on the assumption that I'd benefit as much as he would. In Maths I had a blind spot for algebra, but my spatial sense enabled me to grasp geometry and trigonometry. In Physics I enjoyed conducting experiments with electricity. My form master noted the improvement in my mock exams. Mr Budge noted I'd reached "possible Pass standard in seven subjects and the other two are borderline. He must maintain his efforts in the time remaining." I had no appetite to leave the congenial world of school. In March I completed a "carriers" questionnaire. My mother thought banking might offer a secure job with good prospects, so she encouraged me to attend a talk by a branch manager. In my naivety I was repulsed by the apparent tedium of what the man found so exciting. Following a chat with a Youth Employment Officer I decided, after enjoying Leonard Cottrell's *The Lost Pharoahs* and *The Bull of Minos*, that I'd like to become an archaeologist and dig up lost civilisations. Meanwhile I continued to storm. After the exams my form master noted in the usual end of year report that I'd "worked very well" and hoped my effort "would bring its reward". Mr Budge also "note[d] the improvement this term & trust[ed] that it is not too late." Fear was the spur.

In August the family set off for two weeks holiday in Droskyn Castle, an Edwardian hotel run by the CHA in Perranporth not far from St Ives, perched on a cliff above the village with a view over miles of beach and cliff – the finest setting of all these holidays. My father drove the length of England. We set off at 7.25 and arrived at 12.30 after 17 hours on the road – an epic journey. We had motorway for only a few miles where the A1 bypassed Darlington. My father didn't trust my mother to navigate so he'd apply to the AA for door-to-door directions. He drove slowly and carefully, rarely overtaking or exceeding 40 mph – to my irritation. Vanessa and I sat in the back of the Minx. I don't know how we occupied ourselves. We had no radio – and no music system in distant vinyl days. We'd grown out of I Spy books. We must have chatted. Vanessa and I have always had plenty to say. I shared a room with a couple of boys of my own age. Vanessa shared a room, next door to our parents, with two sisters. One was her age. The other, Judy, was mine.

There must have been ten or a dozen teenagers plus some students among the staff. We formed our own little society, apart from our parents. We visited the sights of far Cornwall – St Michael's Mount, the Lizard, Penzance, Newquay, Hell's Mouth, Marazion and St Ives. We spent time on the beach. We played cards when it rained. We danced to pop records in the evening. In the first week I shared a few kisses with Diane, a quiet 15-year-old. We danced the night before she left. I'd already spent a few hours on the beach at Marazion talking to Judy. She was a Mod princess from Cheltenham, with a Sandie Shaw haircut and a cleft chin like Kirk Douglas'. I might have thought her out of my class. She was already being pursued by John who was a few years older than us, possibly about to start university. On the second Monday we "went on a walk. Talked to Judy most of the day. I quite like her and told she likes me – another likes her – John." Vanessa might have passed on that morsel of inside information from chat in the room she shared with Judy and her sister. On Tuesday we visited St Ives and "danced to Pop records in evening." On Wednesday there was no excursion. We couldn't visit the beach because of rain, so we pulled together a few tables in a bay window overlooking the sea and played cards. I was "pretty sure Judy likes me – but John is spending loads on her." He should have known better with a girl like Judy.

Meanwhile I was waiting for the results of my O Levels. My mother must have arranged for a phone call from school – I think around 6.00 on Wednesday. Anyone who's waited for the result of national exams will know how I felt when I learned I'd passed all nine and had earned grade 1 in four. I could forget about having to find a job – at least for another two years. On Thursday I clinched the deal with Judy. We spent another rainy day playing cards in the lounge. In the evening we watched the usual guests' concert. Afterwards we teens went for a walk: "held Judy's hand after giving John the slip."

The next day, our last, we went on an excursion to Falmouth. I've only memories and entries in my diary for the other girls but, thanks to Vanessa, I've got four photographs of Judy and I on that distant day in August 1965, three taken on the excursion boat and the last in Falmouth. I've placed the third at the head of this chapter. Vanessa took it. I'm at the centre with a complacent smile and hands folded in my lap. Judy's holding her wrist and leaning towards me. John's beside her. The first in the sequence is blurry. I'm sitting against the gunwale with Judy beside me. John's turning to say something with his arm over her shoulders. She's looking straight ahead. I'm solemn. Someone else took the second, because Vanessa, hair cut like Sandie Shaw's, is sitting in front of us, convulsed in laughter. Now it's my arm around Judy, who's looking pissed off while John looks just a bit sheepish. Some irrecoverable incident must have transpired. Vanessa took a last photograph in Falmouth. The youngsters are lined up by a low wall. I'm sitting on the wall behind an older bearded lad, probably a student. I'm laughing towards the camera. My arm's round Judy. She's smiling. John's next to her, looking shrunken.

My diary records that I held Judy's hand most of the day and that we talked on the beach at Falmouth. She'd just been to see the Who. This was before they released 'My Generation'. Then they'd had just a couple of minor hits with 'I Can't Explain' and 'Anyway, Anyhow, Anywhere'. Judy raved about their version of 'Love Hurts'. They never recorded this famous song first recorded by the Everly Brothers but there are a couple of videos on YouTube. One from 1989 features Roger Daltrey performing a pedestrian version backed by a bunch of session musicians not long after the death of Roy Orbison. It's interesting mainly for Daltrey's account of how the group had admired the Big O's version (on the B side of 'Running Scared' from 1961) and would perform it before they became the Who. The second from November 1967 is more interesting. It catches the last 100 seconds of the Who's performance but conveys the full power that Judy must have experienced. She turned me on to the Who. I saw them three times during the next few years. I never saw a better live band. Oddly enough the only other thing I recall is how I explained the origin of the term "bolshie". Who knows what else we talked about?

The day ended the only way it could – in bed in the room Judy shared with her sister and Vanessa, next door to our parents'. Vanessa, a few weeks' short of 13, spent a quiet night in the adjacent bed with one of my roommates (the fair lad you can see leaning in towards me). Judy and I were busier. I record that we remained clothed from the waist down but we'd have had plenty of fun. I'd found my kind of girl – sexually responsive like Judith but intelligent too. I hardly slept and I don't suppose she did. My diary records that I was

165

"dog-tired in the morning – no sleep – petting with Judy all night." I was literally sick from excitement and exhaustion. After saying goodbye and promising to write we drove away in the Hillman, Vanessa and I asleep in the back. We broke the journey at Myf's home in Birmingham and visited Coventry Cathedral. We arrived home on Monday to find that Vanessa's pet rabbit had vanished. It enjoyed a happier fate than Binkie. Vanessa had lost interest in her pet. The rabbit formed an attachment to the cleaner whom it would follow around the house. Our mother invited her to take it home.

The next day, still on holiday, I went into town to buy Judy's favourite record – that reliable floor-filler, the Four Tops' 'I Can't Help Myself'. I wrote to Judy and Diane. At the youth club on the Friday before returning to school in the Sixth form, I enjoyed a barn dance with sweet Marie. On Saturday I had a letter from Judy: "she wants to write – I am very glad." She told me she'd passed seven O Levels, earning a 1 in English, her favourite subject. At school on Monday I discovered the extent of my triumph in the O Level exams. I'd excelled over all but one lad in my form and over most in the top form: "I feel a lot more confident than I did a month ago. Nothing is going wrong at all – I am completely happy – how long will this last?" Remember you are mortal.

SCHOOL PREFECTS 1968

Chapter 10
Point of Departure

1966 was the sixties peak.

(Jon Savage, 1966: The Year the Decade Exploded, 2015)

'Remember how we never went to bed?' somebody said to me in '69, nostalgic already for the '65-'67 era. And it really was a whole era, those two years.

(Andy Warhol and Pat Hackett, POPism: The Warhol Sixties, 1980)

I love being seventeen. Wish I could stay just this age for a while. Seventeen is the perfect spot between that strange state called adolescence, which means you are going somewhere, and adulthood, which means that you are on the downgrade.

(Jon Savage, Teenage: The Creation of Youth Culture, 2007, quoting an anonymous correspondent to an American magazine Seventeen, founded 1944)

My eighteenth year wasn't ending well. I'd excelled in my A-Level subjects (History, Geography, English Literature and Art) but in January 1967 I still hadn't received an offer of a university place. For years History had been my strongest subject but I'd been persuaded to apply to study English by two fine teachers (Watson and Shrimpton). I'd been rejected by Manchester without an interview and by Nottingham – which took me by surprise by asking me to write an appreciation of 'No Swan So Fine' by the American Marianne Moore. Now I can see, what I missed then, that her chintz china swan from the time of Louis Quinze makes an elegant nod to W B Yeats – to the golden bird "set upon a golden bough to sing / To lords and ladies of Byzantium / Of what is past, or passing, or to come" in 'Sailing to Byzantium', and to the wild swans in his poems about Coole Park owned by his friend Lady

Augusta Gregory. I was waiting to hear from my first choice Sussex and from Warwick and East Anglia.

In September I'd visited Hertford College, Oxford, with which the Bede had a connection, for interview along with four other likely lads. I told my diary that I "[g]ave best one at History not English." This interview was conducted by the College's History tutor Felix Markham, one of Napoleon's many biographers. I thought I impressed over a glass of sherry with my grasp of the opening campaigns of the First World War, but was informed a few days later that the College didn't "want me because of the languages" – I lacked the reading knowledge of German and French which I'd need for modern European history, and the Latin needed for medieval history. I'd need to pass Latin O Level (which I'd failed in July and was due to retake in November) and to improve my French and German. I'd have to return to school in the autumn to prepare for the Oxford entrance exam and, if I should succeed, to wait until 1968 before beginning my studies – which sounded a bit of a stretch.

Six years later, at another anxious moment, my mother would tease me for asking her to visit the headmaster Mr Budge for advice on what to do about my lack of an offer of a university place. She must have remembered how I'd taken matters into my own hands as a six-year-old. Sensibly Budge advised that I should do nothing. A few days later I learned that I'd passed Latin O Level at second attempt, opening doors to the many courses that still required Latin (believe it or not). Then I was invited to interviews at Sussex and Warwick, on 14 and 15 February.

I set off on the 13th with David Oliver who'd also applied to study English at Sussex. You can see David second from right in the middle row of the photograph of the Lower Sixth Arts form at the head of the chapter (I'm fourth from right in the front row, beside Graham Mole). He played guitar in the Atoms – and for the school cricket team. I'd known him since we'd been in the same class at Hill View. We all wanted to be invited to parties at his home not far from mine. Together with the formidably clever John

Bowman (in the same class at Hill View) we'd been asked to edit the school magazine *Bedan*. David and John did most of the graft (perhaps that's why they'd kept their places in the A form, unlike me). I'd made my mark in the previous year's edition with a panoramic pen-and-ink drawing of the Battle of Hastings (whose 900th anniversary was commemorated in stamps issued by the General Post Office run by Anthony Wedgwood Benn). I suspect the three of us (with Joe Taylor, one of our party at Hertford) were on the Boys' quiz team that beat the Bede Girls in December. We were the Bede's Bloomsberries. The parallel is piquant. Some of the original Group, like Leonard Woolf, were still living and had been interviewed by Michael Holroyd for his biography of Lytton Strachey, one of the publishing sensations of 1967. Ian Wall enthused over extracts published in *The Sunday Times*. I'd meet Ian and other friends round a table in the Library Tea Rooms – our *Deux Magots* – to talk about life and love. We'd seen Harold Pinter in Sartre's *In Camera* on television and loved Ken Russell's films about Debussy and Isadora Duncan. Ian talked about the Beats and Norman Mailer and Saul Bellow – and nibbled on codeine tablets.

In the mid 1960s Sussex was the most fashionable university in the country, attracting more applicants for each place than Oxford and Cambridge. I haven't been able to find the source but I recall it being described as a hive of hectic heterosexuality. Girls made up about 40% of students, compared to around 30% in all universities. Later I was surprised to learn that it attracted a higher proportion of students from private schools than Oxford or Cambridge. Famously the twin daughters of Douglas Jay, President of the Board of Trade in Harold Wilson's cabinet between 1964 and 1967, attended Sussex and were photographed with him at their graduation in 1966, all long blonde hair and high hem-lines. In 1965 two sixth formers from the Bede had won places to study English at Sussex. Mr Watson encouraged his star pupils to apply.

By 1967, thanks to Beeching, Sunderland had lost its direct rail service to London. David's father must have driven us to the station to catch a train to

Newcastle where we'd change for London. We weren't due to be interviewed until the next day, so we had a few hours to spare before travelling to Brighton. London then was as remote and as glamorous for us as it had been for Billy Fisher in 1963, so we had to take a walk down Carnaby Street in the heyday of "Swinging London" before heading along Oxford Street to the Academy to watch the film version of the celebrated – now notorious – staging of *Othello* with Laurence Olivier in black face.

Othello was the Shakespeare play that we were studying for A Level. This is one of the most disturbing and difficult of his plays. It begins with the veteran soldier Iago complaining about being passed over for promotion by his commanding officer Othello in favour of Cassio, "that never set a squadron in the field", and resolving on revenge. He awakens Brabantio, one of their employers in the Venetian Senate, to tell him that his daughter Desdemona has wed Othello: "Even now, now, very now, an old black ram is tupping your white ewe…. You'll have your daughter covered with a Barbary horse…. I am one, sir, that comes to tell you your daughter and the Moor are now making the beast with two backs."

Try speaking those lines. They must be among the most racially and sexually charged in English literature. The Bede issued its charges with a bowdlerised edition stripped of this kind of language. Mr Shrimpton understood that it was integral to the play and told us to buy our own un-bowdlerised editions. Olivier's production does employ the unexpurgated text but I wonder whether the film will be ever screened again. I suspect that, like *Birth of a Nation*, it's now gone with the wind. I felt some discomfort even then in watching a white man aping what he understood to be the mannerisms of an African. In fact, Olivier's performance was praised precisely for this supposed achievement. Forty years on I watched Lenny Henry play the role in a conventional production faithful to the text, serving to quieten a discomforting memory.

David and I travelled on to Brighton, and visited the university campus the next day for interview. Now it looks across the main road to London towards a monstrous architectural carbuncle in the form of the stadium occupied by Brighton and Hove football club. I'd visited Oxford a few months earlier but had not been charmed. My mother had read Evelyn Waugh's *Brideshead Revisited* when it was published after the war. She borrowed it from Villette Road library for me to read when I was ill at home with flu. I might have read a few pages but it aroused no desire to spend three years in the world evoked by Hertford's best-known alumnus. *Brideshead's* time would come – after the 1960s enthusiasm for modernity had passed.

The last time I visited Sussex University was in August 1997 when I spent a few days with my sons, aged 10 and 7, in a house in the student village, whence we explored Brighton and the Downs and the coast. The campus was already crowded and cluttered with a mass of nondescript buildings. It would have been pristine when David and I approached in February 1967. Designed by Basil Spence, who'd made his reputation as architect of Coventry Cathedral, it was possibly the finest architectural ensemble to be created in Britain since 1945. I described it in my diary as "a lovely place". I preferred Spence's neo-classical modernism on a bright late winter morning to Oxford's autumnal gloom.

David and I would have walked from Falmer station through the tunnel under the A23 and on towards Falmer House, standing as a gate-house to the campus. It had been built as a traditional quadrangle of pre-cast concrete units in-filled with red brickwork. The structure contained hints of Antiquity. Parts had been left empty on the model of the half-ruined Colosseum. At the foot of the inner walls ran a moat surrounding a paved square. David and I would have exited the tunnel under the A23 to London and approached Falmer House along a kind of processional way that entered the quadrangle through one main arch and exited through another after bisecting the paved interior.

As we walked along this way we'd have passed another fragment of moat (now gone) on our right and landscaped lawns on each side. Ahead we'd have seen two concrete pylons flanked by red-brick lecture theatres and beyond them the long, low Arts Building where we were due to be interviewed. To our left on a prominent mound we'd have seen the Library – more neo-classical pre-cast concrete and red brickwork, approached by a long, broad flight of steps. In 1992 I attended a 25th anniversary party for the 1967 student intake at the Groucho Club in Soho. The venue would have been chosen to suit the many media types from my intake. One of them must have brought a print of a film made during the autumn term as part of the 50th anniversary commemoration of the Bolshevik Revolution, with the library steps used to stage a parody of the Odessa Steps sequence in Eisenstein's *Battleship Potemkin*. I was astonished to be pointed out as the officer in command of the troops shooting down the demonstrators. I'd quite forgotten. To our right, masked by a thread of mature trees and with its own moat, we might have noticed the Meeting House. We might even have glimpsed behind it the monumental circular Chemistry lecture theatre, used to stage a student production of *The Trojan Women* one spring evening in 1968. *Et in Arcadia ego.*

I remember nothing of my interview. Afterwards David would have returned to Sunderland while I took the train to Birmingham where I spent the night at Myf's home before taking a bus to Warwick for another interview. I recall only a series of white-tiled blocks, like a public lavatory turned inside out, scattered across a vast, muddy, rain-swept building site. It compared badly with what I'd seen the previous day. No matter: within days we received conditional offers of two Bs from Sussex. I'd gained As in every Sixth form exam and had no worries about the A Level exams. I was on my way – out of Sunderland on a path beaten by the most scholarly children of the town over the decades since then.

Before entering the Sixth form in September 1965 I hadn't given much thought to university. I'd barely looked beyond school. A few careers advice sessions had frightened me about what might lie ahead if I failed to get a decent set of O Levels and had to leave school at 16 as did around half the

Bede lads. Success in passing all my O Levels meant I could forget about my weaker subjects and focus on the ones in which I'd excelled. I surprised myself in the first exams in February 1966 by coming "top in everything – astonishing to see and I hope I don't get big-headed." I did the same in July. I'd earned my place as one of only two Arts pupil to attend Hertford for interview. The prospect of competing for what Lord Birkenhead famously described as "glittering prizes" opened before me. In the same year Vanessa won a transfer to Bede Girls after a year at Barnes, to which she'd been assigned by a rule penalising children born early in the academic year. We seemed to be fulfilling all our parents' hopes.

I returned from Perranporth with even more confidence in my ability to attract girls than after Cromer in 1964. I'd discovered that a bright lad, with a modicum of good looks, could attract girls just as well as sportsmen and musicians. Soon, though, I was suffering the kind of worries that plague all teenagers. One Friday evening a few weeks later on the way home from Ewesley Road youth club I was chagrined to meet friends coming back from one of David Oliver's parties. I lamented: "I wish I could get on better with girls like I do on holiday. Then I wouldn't have such an inferiority complex." I failed to find another Mod princess like Judy – the ones in Sunderland were out of my class. Instead I found the two Paulines, Mullaney and Mullen, both 16, class-mates at West Park Girls Grammar, due to fold into Thornhill Comprehensive about to open near the Bede, itself due to turn comprehensive in 1967. The lower photograph, found through Facebook, shows the Sixth form prefects at Thornhill in 1968. Pauline Mullaney, taller than I recalled, stands on the right at the end of the back row, while Pauline Mullen stands sixth from the left, shy and pretty just like I recall, with long black hair tied in bunches.

These were the last girls whom I met through a church youth club. The one run by Ewesley Road Methodists was my favourite. It didn't host groups like St Nich's. Instead it ran what would soon be called a disco, playing the latest dance records, Motown and Stax now as well as the Rolling Stones and

Beatles. The evenings always ended with a slow dance to the Drifters' 'Save the Last Dance for Me', when even the shy boys, who'd stand by the wall all evening, would try to find a girl. I just have to hear that song, even when mangled by Michael Bublé, and I'm back in Ewesley Road in 1965. This landmark in High Barnes lost its congregation and now stands closed and empty, while a house has been built beside St Nicholas church on the site of the hall where we danced in the 1960s.

I had mixed feelings about Pauline Mullaney, whom I met, probably at Ewesley Road, in late October: "Got a girl!! – not very good but so pleased arranged to see her on Thursday small but not too bad – a good necker." Excuse the wretched syntax – and the awful lack of gallantry – with which I addressed my diary. I was only sixteen. I took Pauline to see Jerry Lewis in *The Disorderly Orderly*. I paid – "10/- gone". I had a more economical evening on Saturday at Ewesley Road and visited her home after church on Sunday. This was our routine for the next couple of months – dances and parties on Fridays and Saturdays, and church on Sunday evening. We'd go back to her home, a new semi-detached house off Silksworth Lane on the way to the colliery, and watch television with her parents for an hour or two before I went home. She held a lively party one Saturday but I had eyes mainly for her blonde friend Erika, who was picked up by Ian Wall – "lucky sod!!" This was the only time I've gone regularly to church. I thought Pauline liked to attend. Later I learned she thought I did. We both wanted to please. Her father was a merchant navy captain. He told me how he'd survived PQ17, deadliest of Arctic Convoys, after the escorts were withdrawn and the convoy was ordered to scatter because of dud intelligence that the giant *Tirpitz*, capable of out-gunning any British warship, was about to make a sortie from its lair in the Norwegian fjords. His hair turned white during a night without darkness in July 1942 as bombers and U-boats closed in on the defenceless merchant ships. Pauline's father was aboard one of only 11 vessels to reach Murmansk out of 35 that left Scotland.

Ours was little more than a boy-girl friendship. We parted amicably on New Year's Eve after beginning the evening at Don Airey's party (which must have been fun) and seeing in the New Year with her parents. Within days she was going out with Ian Wall, now dumped by Erika. The four of us had gone riding a few days earlier, with horses from one of the stables off Newcastle Road. My horse would barely move. It must have eaten too many oats over Christmas. Ian's threw him. Sunderland was like a big village. Pauline and I continued to meet as friends. We saw the Who at the Locarno in 1969 and visited Annabel's night club in 1970 when home from university. I ran into her for the last time in 1977, walking up Pond Street on my way home from the bus terminal at South End Green where I'd catch the No. 24 for Whitehall. She was living in Bethnal Green and about to marry and make a new home in Canada. My mother listened to the bans being read in St Nich's.

I told my diary "I want a really highly sexed girlfriend next, not like Pauline". I'd fancied Erika but soon discovered she wasn't interested. After a couple of fallow months Ian Wall secured an invite to a party that sounded promising. I "asked a girl at the Y.C. to go (Pauline Mullen) – 5' 6" – long black hair – 16 – good looking". I loved her hair – long and glossy like Cher's. I liked her olive skin, the fine black hair on her forearms and the shade of a moustache at the corners of her upper lip. The school photograph reveals a sweet kind face (unlike the diva). She was my first proper girl-friend.

Pauline Mullen lived in a four-storied mid-Victorian house in St Bede's Terrace, just south of Mowbray Park in the oldest part of Ashbrooke. I don't know whether the family occupied the whole house or just part; she never invited me inside. It was fronted by a long path where we'd kiss and cuddle after walking home from the cinema, party or dance in the lengthening spring evenings. This was my Mod phase. I'd wear a black mid-thigh-length double-breasted PVC coat that I'd bought from the Army Surplus shop in Crowtree Road and a John Lennon corduroy cap (in the autumn I'd acquire a parka with fur trim round the hood). Once I'd favoured a tab-collared white shirt (as worn by Mick Jagger) and sometimes a slim black knitted tie. Now

I'd wear a pink or a striped shirt (if possible by Ben Sherman) with a paisley-patterned kipper tie and a pair of hipster trousers bought in West One or Esquire, finished off with a pair of Clarks desert boots. I'd psych myself up with a blast from Dobie Gray before setting out to meet Pauline: "I'm in with the In Crowd / I go where the In Crowd goes." She'd wear her hair long and loose down her back. I took her to see *Alfie, Morgan: A Suitable Case for Treatment, Viva Maria* and *Ice Cold in Alex* and a double bill of Hammer horrors, *Rasputin* and *The Reptile.* We saw *Citizen Kane* at the Empire with tickets that Graham Mole obtained from his mother who worked there.

We'd perch on a pair of high stools in the big picture window of the Bis Bar in Park Lane with the other faces. We'd go to youth club and school dances. In April we saw The Atoms and the Green Onions at the Bede. By now guitar groups were beginning to be supplanted by groups like the Gas Board and Jazz Board with small horn sections allowing them to play Soul songs like Otis Redding's 'Mr Pitiful' or Sam and Dave's 'You Don't Know Like I Know'. The first of the Boards was led by Nigel Olsson and the second by Bryan Ferry, studying Fine Art at Newcastle. Pauline and I went bowling at the Locarno. We sat on the beach at Roker and lay in the grass in Backhouse Park. One evening when the family were out I invited her home: "we necked and petted on the sofa till about 10.30 when she caught the last bus." We'd aim to arrive early at a party so we could bag a bed for a couple of hours of kissing and cuddling before walking home for more of the same in the front garden at St Bede's Terrace. I explored her body like I'd done with Judith and Judy. I felt her excitement as well as my own. One Thursday in April we hosted a party at my home from 7.30 to 11.15 – "seemed to go off quite well." That day I'd bought 'California Dreamin''.

I might say we were teenagers in love, but I never felt confident in her affections. In April I told my diary: "Don't think Pauline likes me very much – not as nice as Mullaney but much better-looking." In May: "I'm always worrying over Pauline – whether or not she really likes me." In June, after we'd been to see Jeanne Moreau and Brigitte Bardot as a pair of gun-toting show-girls in *Viva Maria*: "I think she's going off me though I hope not!" Then, after *Citizen Kane*: "I think I will finish with her soon". The following day: "To finish with Pauline or not to finish with Pauline – that is the question." The following day, 1 July: "Finished with Pauline. Bought '8 miles high' by the Byrds" – presumably by way of consolation or distraction. I suspect I was worrying unnecessarily. She was probably happy enough with me as her boyfriend – just shy about her feelings for an intense youth worrying about whether she'd withdraw her affections. The simplest way to resolve my dilemma was by ending the romance.

I partied on. Parties were what we Sixth formers did. I saw little point in visiting pubs and clubs without money in my pocket and a car in which to drive girls home. I picked up a girl one evening in the Club Astec (not Aztec) in Roker Avenue. She asked if I had a car, and that was it. These parties were innocent enough: a can of IPA or a bottle of Newky (fabled Newcastle Brown Ale), chat with girls and school friends, dancing and maybe a bit of necking and petting. The day after I broke with Pauline Mullen my diary records: "Went to Pauline Mullaney's party – necked a bit with a girl called Hilary 8.45-12.15 quite good". A few days later I was at David Oliver's party: "Monty [that is Graham Mole] took Pauline Mullen home. I got no one". I was at another party when England beat Portugal in a World Cup semi-final. Over the next few days there were three more parties. Then on Saturday 30 June I joined my father to watch England beat West Germany in the Final. My mother brought tea while we waited for the game to resume for a last half-hour. We were exhausted when it was over. I recalled the occasion at my father's funeral, like so many sons must have done.

I remained on good terms with my second Pauline like I did with my first. A few years later she invited me to a New Year's Eve party at the flat she shared with her husband. Not long afterwards I ran into her pushing a pram with the first of four children. When I visited the North East with my family in 1996 we spent a few days with Graham Mole and his family. He told me that Pauline was running a B&B not far away in Thornhill Gardens. He said she still remembered me. Chris Pike told me he'd stayed at her B&B about ten years later when visiting his widowed mother still living in Stannington Grove. He reminded Pauline discreetly about the last time he'd seen her – in bed with me at one of his parties. She'll never be able to read these lines; in 2009 she was hit by a car on an evening out and fatally injured. She wasn't yet 60.

Someone else who'll no longer be able to read these lines is Graham Mole, who'd taken Pauline home a few evenings after we parted. Sunderland was indeed a village. Graham's younger brother Ian has written at length about his family in a series of memoirs. Their father was born in Blyth and joined the merchant navy as an apprentice after leaving school at 15 in 1930. Graham told me he'd helped to run guns to the Republicans during the Spanish Civil War, under threat of attack by Italian bombers and submarines. Ian tells how he qualified as a merchant seaman gunner just before the war. He helped to evacuate soldiers from Dunkirk and served aboard colliers along the eastern coast as well as on Atlantic and Arctic convoys. He was rescued when one ship was sunk by mine. Another ship survived a torpedo attack. On the way to Murmansk he shot down a Dornier bomber circling to attack his ship after having just sent another to the bottom, consigning the crew to an icy sea. After the war he served as a second officer aboard colliers. He met Graham's mother when she was on holiday near Blyth while still in her teens. They married in 1948. Graham was born in 1949. Linda and Ian followed a few years later. In 1956 Graham's father left the sea for a job as a progress chaser in an engineering factory. His mother had trained as a typist and worked as secretary to the director of the Empire Theatre.

When I met Graham the family was living mainly on the ground floor of a terraced house owned by his maternal grandmother which they shared with a series of lodgers, including Iraqi students at the Tech. Not until 1965 could his parents afford to buy their own house nearby in Otto Terrace. Graham and I had bonded over pop music; we were both terrible music snobs. Neither of us had the patience to learn to play guitar or we'd have formed a group. Instead we'd play fantasy groups – we'd debate the line-up of our imaginary group and devise set lists. He's sitting beside me in the photograph at the head of this chapter showing the lower Sixth Arts form in May 1966, taken at the height of my romance with Pauline Mullen.

Classmates noticed our affinity. We were casual, unthinking homophobes, though the term had yet to be invented. In January my diary records: "I am being called a puff at school – stupid buggars – I'm no puff nor is Monty." That's not to say I didn't worry about our friendship. In March, just before I started seeing Pauline Mullen, I complain that he's "getting possessive again, damn." A few days later: "I must get rid of Mole – he's making me rely on him all the time – I must break away from his influence." Then: "My sex-life is likely to remain stagnant until I get a friend who likes girls: unlike Mole. Is he a puff???" Of course he wasn't, maybe just a bit of a late developer, born in August. He was as girl-mad as I was.

Graham was my closest friend during the rest of my time at the Bede. We'd visit the cinema together. We jumped out of our seats in the Picture House when hands shot from the walls of a South Kensington flat to grab Catherine Deneuve as her mind disintegrates in Roman Polanski's *Repulsion*: "an excellent horror film – best I've ever seen". I'd say the same today, after several further viewings. We enjoyed the Burton and Taylor double act in *Who's Afraid of Virginia Woolf?* but were disappointed by *Beat Girl* from 1961 and starring Adam Faith at the height of the Trad Boom. In my diary I dismissed what was once thought daring as "a complete anachronism" – from before the invention of sexual intercourse. Nothing dates so quickly as the self-consciously edgy.

Graham had impeccable taste in music. I don't mean simply that we liked the same records – though generally we did. We especially liked records that were "subtle" and "powerful." The Byrds and the Lovin' Spoonful usually passed that test. He must have passed on his taste for the Lovin' Spoonful to Ian, who recalls that his first purchase was 'Summer in the City' in 1966.

Graham had an unerring ear for gems like 'Kelly' on the B side of Del Shannon's 'Hats off to Larry'. He could spot overlooked R&B tracks like the Essex's 'Easier said than done'. We loved the Trashmen's eccentric 'Surfin' Bird' and the Bobby Fuller Four's version of 'I fought the law', penned by Sonny Curtis who took the place of Buddy Holly in the Crickets and recorded the song in 1959. In the early 1970s we despised Prog Rock and loved self-destructive Gram Parsons, blazing like a meteor through rock music from the moment in 1968 when he joined the Byrds in place of David Crosby, through his friendship with Keith Richards and his exquisite duets with Emmylou Harris, until his death in 1973 from a drug over-dose and his immolation by the roadside in Joshua Tree Desert. There was something of Gram about Graham.

His mother was able to obtain free tickets for shows at the Empire. That's how he got to see the Beatles when they performed there twice in 1963 – much to my envy. A visit to the Empire to see the pantomime was a regular part of Christmas as a child. I must have seen some of the last stars of music hall, like Max Wall strutting in his black tights. Now I started to visit the Empire regularly with Graham. We enjoyed classics like *Macbeth, Henry V, Richard II, The Tempest, Romeo and Juliet* and *Volpone* but were most impressed by David Halliwell's *Little Malcolm and his struggle against the eunuchs* and *Brasiliana 67*.

Halliwell's play was a one-off. He never wrote anything like it again. Mike Leigh described him as a true bohemian rather than a latter-day beatnik or proto-hippie. Leigh directed a six-hour version at the Unity Theatre in 1965 but another director cut it down to two and half hours for brief runs in 1966 in the West End and on Broadway, with John Hurt in the title role. This was the version that Graham and I watched in 1967, mounted by the National Youth Theatre – without Hurt but including Helen Mirren, aged 21, as the object of Malcolm Scrawdyke's desire. Looking back from 2011 she dismissed it as a typical Angry Young Man play of the sixties. As with all those plays, it was a boy's fantasy and the girl's role was sexist crap. However, it was a professional engagement, with a wage attached. We played for a week at the Empire, Sunderland. The vast, echoing mausoleum of an auditorium seated around two thousand. We attracted around two hundred. The seats of the theatre were like cinema seats; they flipped noisily up if someone stood to leave. More people took that option, especially when I had to deliver the line 'Will you shaft me?' By the end of the play there were maybe a hundred and thirty-four left in the audience.

It would have included Graham and me on Wednesday 22 February.

La Mirren is striving for an easy laugh. She must have known that the Angry Young Men like John Osborne had written in the 1950s. Graham and I had no difficulty in grasping that Halliwell's play was about the psychological roots of extremist politics. As a failed art student expelled from college who enrols three friends in his Party of Dynamic Erection and persuades them to raise their arms to salute him with "Hail Scrawdyke", Malcolm obviously looks back to Hitler – but also forwards to the student revolutionaries of the late 1960s, to the Red Army Fraction and Symbionese Liberation Army of the 1970s; and to today's bedsit jihadis and incels. *Brasiliana 67* was something completely different: "lovely young negresses in brief bikinis – cor!!!"

Graham and I had our difficulties. Neither was ready to defer to the other when we went out hunting girls. They seemed always to come in pairs: a pretty one whom we both fancied and her "plug mate" whom neither would accept. That master of misanthropy Patrick Hamilton put his finger on this peculiarity, which must be as much of a bone of contention now as a hundred years ago in Brighton.

> It might be supposed that normally a pretty girl would pair with a pretty girl, and a plain one with a plain one. But such is not the case. Owing to some mystifying law of psychology or expediency, couples of this sort are more often than not composed of such opposites, and this law has always been as dismaying as it is mystifying to those young men who are also walking in pairs and desiring to talk to girls. Who is to take, to put up with, to be palmed off with, the 'other one'?

Graham would have recognised the situation at once. We would have laughed as we recalled the way neither of us would defer to the other – to be Hamilton's 'other one', whose "business [is] to take, to put up with, be palmed off with the 'other one' on the other side." I found a more biddable "tapping partner" (wingman in today's parlance) in one Charles Ernest Brown with whom I visited clubs and dances before and after my time with the first Pauline.

All who knew Graham will recall his streak of mischief, even malice. One evening, when we were in my bedroom listening to records, he tried to pinch the five-year diary from which I've been quoting. His brother tells how he pulled the same trick on him. In early 1967 I describe him behaving like Iago in *Othello*, trying to poison my mind with jealousy about some girl. I complained to my diary about his "contemptuous attitude towards me". By the time I set off for university we'd smoothed over these petty frictions and overcome the Hamilton problem by finding a pair of pretty girls: me with one of Sunderland's It girls, blonde Jill Roumph ("comfy Roumphy"), and Graham with her equally attractive friend, dark Helen Fleuret – two more people who'll never read these pages.

Graham never found a proper outlet for his talents. He was a fine linguist but did poorly in his first shot at A Levels and returned for a third year in the Sixth form after his friends had left. He did well enough this time around to find a place through clearing to study Classics at Hull University, but left after two terms. After a few months behind the wheel of a butcher's delivery van, he found a job as a work-study man in the NHS. In 1974 he ditched Helen who left for London where we met a couple of times. I lost touch with Graham and didn't see him again until I visited the North East in 1996. By then he'd been married for 20 years to Gill, whom he'd met after breaking with Helen Fleuret. Both worked for the NHS until they left for Saudi Arabia in 1977 to work in a private hospital in Jeddah on the coast of the Red Sea. They enjoyed plenty of unauthorised drinking and learned to wind-surf. In 1983 they returned to Sunderland with big savings. In 1996 they were living in a four or five-storied end-of-terrace house overlooking Ashbrooke rugby ground. Graham was restoring the house and collecting "vintage" (out of date) sound systems while Gill worked as an NHS art therapist. They had a son and daughter a few years older than my sons. He showed me round town and tried to teach me wind-surfing in an artificial lake on land reclaimed from a defunct colliery.

Things had fallen apart when I saw him again, for the last time, in 2004. Graham's marriage ended around the same time as mine. The grand house had gone and Graham was living with his mother when I called – with just my sons this time. Graham's father died in 1981 and his mother married again. Now she was nursing her second husband as he lay dying, with Graham sleeping on a camp bed. He and Gill were arguing over the division of assets from the marriage. We had lunch at the Rosedene and took a walk by the sea at Seaburn. We kept in intermittent touch by text and phone. He was surprised that I didn't win a higher score with my special subject of LA rock music from the Byrds to the Eagles when I appeared on *Mastermind* in 2006. I've kept an old Nokia with Graham's last text, from 13 July 2012. I'd asked whether he intended to see Bruce Springsteen in concert at the Stadium of Light (no prizes for guessing what he'd have called it): "if I wanted to see a 62 yr old failed superstar I'll look in the fucken mirror". Some time afterwards I had an uncanny sense when I glanced at his words that the author, to whom I'd once been so close, was no longer among us. Out of the blue I received an email from Judith Wall telling me that Graham had died from chronic lung disease in January 2014. He must have been too proud to tell me he was ill.

A week after finishing with Pauline Mullen, about a dozen lads studying English in the lower Sixth paid a visit to Keele University for a conference organised by the Critical Quarterly Society. The aim was to offer a taste of university life to pupils considering whether to study English. We arrived on Monday. On Tuesday we deigned to attend what I described as a "boring lecture". In the afternoon we withdrew to the snooker room where we monopolised the tables for the rest of the week. We held a party until 1.00 am on the first night. On the second we ran a card school until 2.30 am from which I came away with winnings of two shillings. On the last evening I relaxed with Deidre: "hell of a lover – in my bedroom till 3.30." I was bowled over by this taste of what I took to be student life. I "came home in a raging temper for various reasons" – reasons I failed to understand and couldn't begin to analyse in the space available in my diary. I escaped to the end-of-year dance at the Bede where the Junco Partners, the top local group, playing a guitar-driven R&B that was starting to slip from fashion, were performing. I was in no mood to pick up a girl.

Now I encountered the novel that, more than any other, would help me to understand my turbulent feelings. People born in the two decades after 1945 were probably the last to whom the early novels of D H Lawrence would make sense. Sunderland was still a big ship-building town, with a colliery not far from the town centre (where the Stadium of Light stands now) and other pits in the surrounding villages. In an interview in 2014 Don Airey recalled growing up in Ashbrooke.

> I remember waking up each morning at 7.30 to the sequence of shipyard buzzers summoning the faithful to work – it was like a symphony. We'd sometimes stay in the school bus all the way back into town, just to watch the thousands of men pouring out of the yards and up the High Street when work was over.

When leaving St Nich's, near the road from town to the colliery village of Silksworth a few miles away, we'd take care to avoid tanked-up young miners on the way home from drinking in the town centre pubs. As in Lawrence's day, we'd been raised by stay-at-home mothers, without the labour-saving devices like washing machines and fridges that began to arrive only in the late 1950s. Second-wave feminism didn't begin until the early 1970s. The idea of the "family wage" that a man needed to support a wife and children remained current in the 1980s. A girl who fell pregnant in the 1960s would either marry the father, like Virginia Garnett married Peter Bottomley and went on to serve in John Major's cabinet, or would give up her baby for adoption, like Clare Short who resigned from Tony Blair's.

In the lower Sixth we'd read Robert Graves's *Goodbye to All That* and Joseph Conrad's *Nostromo*. During the summer of 1966 I read Lawrence's *Sons and Lovers* before studying it in the autumn. At first I wasn't impressed. I dismissed the author as "a nonentity compared to Conrad's genius." Soon the novel began to make sense. Raymond Williams, son of a railway worker in Welsh border country, gets it right when he observes how *Sons and Lovers* explores the tension between the "sense of close quick relationship [in] the life of the family in a small house" (like the ones in which Williams and Lawrence and I grew up) and the urge for liberation, something beyond personal happiness, which Lawrence portrays in Paul Morel and which I'd begun to feel. Paul's affairs with Miriam and Clara were beyond an emotional horizon which I didn't begin to approach until my last confused weeks with Pauline Mullen: "I like P. too much to want to hurt her yet am sexually attracted to her so do not want to know about sexual intercourse which could possibly occur in the next month or so". I was struggling to find words for unfamiliar feelings.

More resonant was Lawrence's account of Paul Morel's relationship with his mother. As I sensed about my own mother, Mrs Morel had married a handsome man who was her social and intellectual inferior. She'd become disappointed in him and channelled thwarted hopes into her son Paul. I too sensed in my mother "something so hard and certain..., as if she never had a misgiving in her life." Mrs Morel had married for passion, just as I thought my mother had done, but she can still tell Paul: "I've never had a husband." My father, unlike Paul's, was a constantly gentle man; but the cultural and intellectual gulf between my parents was no smaller. I felt that my mother was embarrassed by her husband's gaucherie. Perhaps that's why they never entertained friends in their home. Like Paul, I bore the weight of a mother's "great belief" in her son, "the more because he was unaware of his own powers. There was so much to come out of him. Life for her was rich with promise. She was to see herself fulfilled. Not for nothing had been her struggle." Like Paul Morel I felt I'd had to "fight against" my mother to assert my independence. I began to hear my mother's voice in Mrs Morel's words, as when she tells Paul how she wants him only to be happy: "But damn your happiness," he responds. "So long as life's full, it doesn't matter whether it's happy or not. I'm afraid your happiness would bore me." The words struck a chord.

I felt I was marking time. I was hungry for a sexual relationship but couldn't imagine conducting one while I was living at home under the eyes of my parents. I was looking ahead to university. I couldn't imagine settling into a marriage and family life in my home town – like Pauline Mullen and other girls whom I'd met. I was bored by my last family holiday in Dawlish and brushed off the nice ordinary girl who pursued me. As I entered my final year at school I quickly found that I'd left youth clubs behind. "Went to Ewesley Rd Y.C. – only about 30-40 there at the most. Last year there was 70-80 average". In November I went to a "crap St Nich's dance. Those there reminded me of two years ago when I went." Now I'd visit the Barnes pub, where I'd nurse a half or a pint while chatting to school friends. I started going regularly to the Bay Hotel in Seaburn, where the ultra-violet lighting would pick out every speck of dust or fragment of dandruff on my black velvet-cord jacket. I went regularly to dances at the Tech College in Chester Road on a Saturday night where the Brian Auger Trinity with Julie Driscoll performed regularly. I was too young for the girls. In January I "asked about 6 birds – no luck". After a dance in May I noted that "[n]one of the 10 Bede lads there got a bird." I attended plenty of parties and took out a few girls, but found no special one.

My appetite for university was whetted by a second "taster" course at Manchester University in January 1967. This time I attended the lectures. I met "quite a good-looking girl" called Jane. On the final evening we took a bus into the city centre through dark, slushy streets to see David Lean's *Dr Zhivago* – "very good film". Imagine the impact it must have made as we watched Julie Christie and Omar Sharif riding in their sleigh under a bright sky on the way to ice-bound Varykino while 'Lara's Theme' soars on the soundtrack. We would have been well-primed for a few hours in bed – the usual necking and petting, still learning the game, learning how to enjoy one another without compulsion to go straight to number one. The film offered a more potent image of revolution than Villon and his ruffians: the black leather-coated, bespectacled commissar Strelnikov (literally Shooter) as portrayed by Tom Courtenay, seated behind a desk in an armoured train and expounding on the need to sacrifice personal life in the service of history.

All the while during this last year at school I was building the intellectual muscle on which I've relied since then. Three times I scaled the heights of Henry James' *The Ambassadors*. I studied 19th century British and European history under supervision from the finest scholar among our teachers, "Fuzzy" Waites, who taught history, politics and economics only to the upper Sixth and regularly despatched a squad of pupils to the LSE. He treated me like an undergraduate, setting essay topics and guiding my reading and discussing my essays. I read current histories of modern France and Russia, and A J P Taylor on the course of German history, Bismarck and the struggle for mastery in Europe ending in the First World War. I developed my own ideas about the origins of the war, focussing on Russia. I was reading George Dangerfield's *The Strange Death of Liberal England* in the cinema as the lights went down for *The Blue Max*. I was laying the foundations for a degree in History, even though I'd been accepted by Sussex to study English.

I put girls to one side as I revised for a month or so ahead of the A Level exams which posed a lesser challenge than either O Levels or Finals three years later. Afterwards I enjoyed the Summer of Love. The day after my last exam I "[b]ought 'Respect' by Aretha Franklin by way of celebrating the end of A-levels". One evening I lost the PVC coat I'd worn on evenings with Pauline Mullen, with the scarf given by Pauline Mullaney at Christmas 1965 in its pocket, stolen from the cloakroom during a dance at the Teacher Training College in Langham Towers, a converted Victorian mansion in

Ryhope Road. One evening at the Bay I met a girl whom I took to a party at David Oliver's to celebrate the end of A Levels. The Beatles had just released *Sergeant Pepper*, which played on repeat. There were more dances as the school year ended – and another girl. Together with Ian Wall and his girl we made a foursome when he drove to Durham and Finchale Priory. Ian was the only one of my friends to own a car, bought by his father who'd become a partner in Sunderland's main estate agency. Often at weekends we'd drive around hunting for parties. I spent an idle week as a hospital porter, reading *The Daily Telegraph* most of the time. My mother worked in the Benefits section of the Department of Health and Social Security (based in Phoenix House by the main station). She explained how to claim Supplementary Benefit. Mainly, though, I sat in the garden and read. I found little in Aldous Huxley's *The Doors of Perception*, which famously inspired the Doors, but read straight through, often into the early hours, three pristine volumes of *Lord of the Rings* from Villette Road.

In August I revisited Cromer for a couple of weeks' holiday with Phil Smith (fifth from right in the middle row in the photograph) as a companion. Phil was a bright lad (he won the school prize for History) with good taste in music (as a pioneer Beach Boys fan), but he was a dull companion whom I soon shook off to spend time on the beach and in bed with a precociously sexy 14 year-old. I've kept the photograph of Heather posing on the lawn at home in a bikini that she sent afterwards. A few years later, bored with marriage, she wrote inviting an affair – an offer which I didn't take up. I was enchanted by the scientist daughter of a Jewish Communist lecturer in Mathematics from London's East End with a plausible claim to have fought Oswald Mosley's fascists as a young man in the 1930s. The peak of festivities came in early September. Scott Mackenzie's 'If you're going to San Francisco' had just been supplanted from No. 1 by Engelbert Humperdinck's 'The Last Waltz'. Chris Pike threw a memorable party. We took over his house for a couple of hours while his parents were out. He tells me the piano was never the same after someone spilt a pint of Black Velvet (cider and stout) inside it.

Lads ran up and down the road plucking flowers from gardens and throwing them over one another – flower power, Sunderland-style. Then Chris was off to sea for a disastrous few weeks.

We tend to forget that the summer of 1967 was also a summer of war and revolution. Then I still took my politics from my mother, who'd join the Monday Club in the aftermath of Enoch Powell's notorious "Rivers of Blood" speech. I'm embarrassed (but obliged) to admit that my diary records in November 1965 that "I'm all behind [Ian] Smith on Rhodesia". The following October I record that I "[p]roposed the motion in the 6th Form Society tonight on the subject of integration". I didn't need to spell out what line I took. David Oliver recalled in his report on the event in the *Bedan* that Ian Wall and I had argued for segregation as "the only solution to the racial problem", but had been defeated by John Bowman and another lad who argued against us. In June 1967, just as I took my first A Level exam, I rejoiced in Israel's lightning victory: "I am delighted Israel thrashed Nasser's Arabs." I'd been reading my parents' *Daily Mail*. I'd form a more measured view after reading Maxime Rodinson's Penguin Special *Israel and the Arabs* in 1968. In 1965 I'd been impressed by the decisive way in which Lyndon Johnson committed tens of thousands of troops to the war in Vietnam. I'd read about the French in Vietnam in Larteguy's *The Centurions*. I must have assumed that the Americans would prevail where the French had failed. By the summer of 1967 they'd descended into a similar morass. Protests were mounting and ghettoes were burning. I must have been drawing a contrast with Israel's lightning victory when I wrote – in egregious teenage solipsism – a couple of days later: "I am fed up with the Vietnam War now". Notoriously the skies began to darken as the decade neared its end.

I learned my A level results over the phone while in Cromer. Grade A in English, History and Geography and D in Art (I'd done poorly in the History of Art paper for which I did little revision) was more than enough to secure a place at Sussex. David Oliver failed to get the grades he needed, so I'd have to go there on my own. Now I faced the dilemma of whether to accept my place at Sussex or to try for St John's College, Cambridge, with which the Bede had the same kind of connection as with Hertford College and the LSE.

My mother wanted me to try for Cambridge but my instinct was for Sussex: "I hate the idea of spending another year in Sunderland which I will have to do if I go to Cambridge in 1968". Ties of sentiment weakened after we moved to a bigger semi-detached house just before A Levels. I'd enjoyed school but now I'd had enough. I wanted to leave home. I didn't fancy spending another term at school while I prepared for the Cambridge entrance exam and then marking time in a dull job in Sunderland. I lacked the adventurous spirit for overseas travel. I discussed the options with Mr Budge and "Fuzzy" Waites who ran the connection with St John's as well as LSE. Ian Wall and I had befriended Steve Winters, a precocious Fifth former who put me in touch with his elder brother David who'd been accepted by Sussex to study English in 1965. The decision was complicated after I became involved with Jill Roumph, whom I thought could choose any lad she wanted. Somewhere I still have a photograph of her with short blonde hair and wearing a tight sweater and miniskirt. She offered a good reason to spend a further year in Sunderland. I tried to secure the promise of a place from St John's, like one lad had done, but they refused: I'd have to sit the exam. I wasn't prepared to gamble. I plumped for Sussex on the Thursday before the Monday I was due to start. On Sunday my parents drove Jill and me to Newcastle where they waved me off on the train to London.

I've often wondered how life would have turned out if I'd plumped for Cambridge. Almost certainly I'd have passed the entrance exam. But the ancient universities held no appeal. A born rebel who'd loved Hiawatha and thrilled to Villon at the head of his band of vagabonds, the teenage lad who'd chased girls compulsively and obsessed over pop music, was unlikely to thrive in a more traditional, largely male setting. For better or worse I was always going to choose Sussex.

EPILOGUE
On Wilbury Hill

An aged man is but a paltry thing, / A tattered coat upon a stick, unless / Soul clap its hands and sing, and louder sing / For every tatter in its mortal dress

(W B Yeats, 'Sailing to Byzantium', 1928)

Yeats was in his early 60s – ten years younger than me but in valetudinarian mood – when he published 'Sailing to Byzantium'. He'd always been a handsome man and was now a distinguished (if somewhat portly) one – "a sixty-year-old smiling public man" in his famous line from 'Among School Children', conducting a school inspection as a member of the Irish Senate. He had eleven years to live.

Like Orwell, Yeats wrote partly as a way of overcoming mortality: "gather me / Into the artifice of eternity", he commands the "sages standing in God's holy fire" whom he invokes. But he finds his subjects in the "dying generations" that "commend all summer long / Whatever is begotten, born and dies", neglecting the "Monuments of unageing intellect" celebrated by the ageing poet.

I began to compose this memoir in June 2020 while walking on Wilbury Hill, west of Letchworth, looking over the valley of the Hiz towards Hitchin. I've been taking this walk regularly since my then wife and I moved from London to Letchworth with our first son in 1989, while she was pregnant with our second lad. I'd been taking this walk most days since lockdown began in March. By the end of August I'd finished a first draft, which I put aside as I resumed my teaching at the business school.

I'd walk for 15 minutes through the streets towards Wilbury Hill with a sense of mounting anticipation. As I reached the edge of town I'd cross a road and take the track to the left of the Wilbury pub. Brambles and nettles close in on the track during summer. To maintain social distance I'd need to make way for someone walking towards me. After a few hundred yards I'd reach the end of this path and ahead the prospect would open as in the photograph. I'd already decided to conclude with an account of this walk.

I'd step out along a stretch of the Icknield Way which begins near Bury St Edmunds and runs beyond Letchworth along the crest of the Chilterns to Princes Risborough. People have been walking these paths for thousands of years. On my left I'd look across a field of ripening corn towards Hitchin and the hills behind it. On my right I'd look through gaps in a straggling whitethorn hedge towards the flooded quarry where once I'd swum and to trees masking a new housing estate in the grounds of a former Victorian mental hospital. Ahead on the far horizon I'd see the Delectable Mountains where Christian found relief before setting off for his final destination.

Soon the hedge on my right would give way to a small covert of woodland preserved for foxes and game birds. In 2020, while exploring this covert, I found a broken bunker that a vagrant must have built. Beyond the covert the prospect opens in all directions, from the Chilterns across the Vale of Bedford towards the hills that Christian climbed after vanquishing Apollyon.

Soon the main path descends towards the Hiz. Invariably I'll take a sharp left turn downhill, shading my eyes against the setting sun on a winter afternoon. That summer I'd catch the scent from the big lavender field on my left that's been attracting visitors for the last 15 years. Past the lavender field I'd walk between farm buildings and make a second sharp left turn along a clay path past stables on my right. Beyond the stables, horses graze in paddocks. In winter or after rain the path turns muddy and pitted with puddles. After passing between small stands of trees it reaches a T-junction with the main Icknield Way. I'll turn left towards home.

On my left the land rises. I see the tips of pines on the horizon in front of me. On my right I'll look across a wide field towards the embankment carrying the railway between Hitchin and Letchworth. In spring and summer I might stop to scan the sky for an ascending skylark. Occasionally throughout the year I might spy a kite. Soon, as the ground rises, the path acquires a hedge on the right and a few trees straggle on the left as it climbs towards the pines and the streets leading home. The circuit takes about half an hour – unless I stop to chat, as I often did during that first lockdown when the circuit attracted more than the usual number of walkers.

Typically I'd make this walk in the late afternoon. I'd compose in my head as I walked. I might laugh out loud if I hit on just the right word or phrase. When I arrived home I'd read for a time or potter in the garden. I'd start cooking dinner as the Radio 4 news began at 6.00. I'd have washed up and finished my coffee by 7.30.

I'd open the computer and cast my mind back to when I played on Roker Beach or roamed Tunstall Hill – like John Lilburne must have done, a few decades before John Bunyan walked the Bedford hills and vales I can see from Wilbury Hill.

NOTES ON SOURCES

Apart from memory and conversation with my sister Vanessa, this memoir draws mainly on a mass of disordered papers – letters, newspaper cuttings and assorted documents – plus photographs, loose and in albums, that I've inherited from my parents and grandparents. For the last three chapters I've drawn heavily on diaries that I began keeping in January 1962 when I was about to turn 13. At various points I've drawn on other sources listed below.

xiii   For 'ego-documents' see Alison Light, *Common People: The History of an English Family*, 2014.

xiv   The third of Ian Mole's volumes of reminiscence of his youth is *Ling Hong Blues*, 2019 (the reference is to a local Chinese restaurant) after *Tiddle-Ee-Aye-Go*, 2017 and *Michelle My Umbrella*, 2018.

1   For Bunyan's military service see Christopher Hill, *A Turbulent, Seditious, and Fractious People. John Bunyan and his Church*, 1988. For the way children read Bunyan see Jonathan Rose, *The Intellectual Life of the British Working Classes*, 2001.

3   Richard Thompson (with Scott Timberg), *Beeswing: Fairport, Folk Rock and Finding my Voice 1967-75*, 2021.

4   Kim Philby, *My Silent War*, 1969.

10   For the sea as a dangerous calling see Dan Jackson, *The Northumbrians: North-East England and Its People: A New History*, 2019.

11   John Darwin, *Unlocking the World: Port Cities and Globalization in the Age of Steam, 1830-1930*, 2021.

13   For TB see Juliet Gardiner, *The Thirties: An Intimate History*, 2010 and Light, *Common People*.

16   For shipbuilding and coal exports see Darwin, *Unlocking the World*.

20   W S Churchill, *The Second World War II: Their Finest Hour*, 1949. The words are frequently quoted.

26   For ports in India and China see Darwin.

33   R F Foster, *W B Yeats: A Life II. The Arch-poet*, 2003 contains a good account of Sato's gift.

40 John Terraine, *Business in Great Waters: The U-Boat Wars 1916-1945*, 1988 and Jonathan Dimbleby, *The Battle of the Atlantic: How the Allies Won The War*, 2015 contain accounts of the Laconia incident. There's a Wikipedia entry for Heinrich Liebe.

50 For Board Schools see Nicholas Timmins, *The Five Giants. A Biography of the Welfare State*, 1996, and Chris Renwick, *Bread for All. The Origins of the Welfare State*, 2018. For Westoe Road School see J A Graham, 'The South Shields School Board 1871-1903', a thesis submitted in 1964 for the degree of Master of Education at Durham University. For an appreciation of these schools see Rose, *Intellectual Life*.

52 Butcher's apprentice quoted in Gardiner, *The Thirties*.

55 For cars on the road in the 1930s see Gardiner. For homosexuality see Noel Annan, *Our Age: The Generation That Made Post-war Britain*, 1990.

59 Details of Aberaeron County School from a history published in 1951 to mark the opening of the present much larger school next door to the original building. I owe this reference to Margaret Jones, Ceredigion Archives.

60 For A Levels in 1955 see Richard Layard, John King and Claus Moser, *The impact of Robbins*, 1969.

61 Jon Savage, *Teenage: The Creation of Youth Culture 1875-1945*, 2007.

63 Churchill quoted in Dimbleby, *The Battle of the Atlantic*.

68 Max Weber, 'The Social Psychology of the World Religions', in H H Gerth & C Wright Mills (eds), *From Max Weber: Essays in Sociology*, 1948.

71 For package holidays see Dominic Sandbrook, *States of Emergency. The Way We Were: Britain 1970-1974*, 2011.

85 N Pevsner, *The Buildings of England: County Durham*, 1953. I'm grateful to Alan Hooper for the gift of this book.

87 Michael Young's interviewee quoted in David Kynaston, *Family Britain 1951-57*, 2009.

88 Georg Lukacs, *Record of a Life*, 1983

89 Jon Savage, *Teenage*.

96 For housing classes see John Rex and Robert Moore, *Race, Community and Conflict: A Study of Sparkbrook*, 1967 and for Cutteslowe see Gardiner, *The Thirties*. For Stevenson's map see John Rowe Townsend, *Written for Children. An Outline of English-language Children's Literature*, 1965.

97 Raban quote from *Soft City*, 1974.

118 Nik Cohn, *AwopBopaLooBop AlopBamBoom: Pop from the Beginning*, 1969.

121 David Kynaston, *Modernity Britain 1957-62*, 2013.

123 Sutherland quoted in Kynaston, *Family Britain.*

128 Biographical details of Plievier from Dieter Sevin, 'Theodor Plievier's Double Exile in Russia', *Colloquia Germanica*, 10:2, 1976-77 and John Willetts, *The New Sobriety: Art and Politics in the Weimar Period 1917-33*, 1978.

130 For the BBC play see Oliver Wake, 'Stalingrad (1963)' on the website British Television Drama. There's a Wikipedia entry for Rudolph Cartier.

132 For *The Eagle* see Dominic Sandbrook, *Never Had It So Good: A History of Britain from Suez to the Beatles*, 2005.

135 Wikipedia entry for Hugo Pratt.

139 Juliet Nicolson, *Frostquake. The frozen winter of 1962 and how Britain emerged a different country*, 2021;

140 Wikipedia entry for Tony Meehan.

145 For Buddy Holly see Howard Sounes, *Down the Highway: The Life of Bob Dylan*, 2001; Ian MacDonald, *Revolution in the Head: The Beatles' Records and the Sixties*, 1995; and Keith Richards (with James Fox), *Life*, 2010.

151 Statistics from Speech Day programmes for 1965 and 1967. For national statistics see Layard *et al*, *The impact of Robbins*. For Nigel Olsson see the interview in *Rolling Stone*, August 22, 2018.

153 For the contraceptive pill see Sandbrook, *States of Emergency.*

155 Nick Hornby, *High Fidelity*, 1995.

159 For the Jaynetts see Jon Savage, *1966: The Year the Decade Exploded*, 2015.

171 For percentages of male and female students at Sussex and across the sector see David Daiches (ed), *The idea of a new university: An experiment in Sussex*, 1964 (I'm grateful to Alan Hooper for the loan of this book) and House of Commons, *Education: Historical Statistics*, 2012.

173 For Spence's intentions see his contribution to Daiches, *The idea of a new university.*

176 For PQ17 see Dimbleby, *The Battle of the Atlantic.*

178 For Bryan Ferry see Michael Bracewell, *Remake/Re-model. The Art School Roots of Roxy Music*, 2007. I was astonished when Graham Mole told me in 1996 that Ferry had fronted the Gas Board whom we'd seen in youth clubs.

180 For Graham and his family see Ian Mole (with his mother) *That's All I Can Tell Yer*, 2020 and *Off to the Bish!*, 2021.

182 There's a Wikipedia entry for David Halliwell, with a link to Matt Trueman, 'Mike Leigh on David Halliwell: "He's one of the great writers who never happened"', *The Guardian*, 7 July 2015. Helen Mirren quote from *In the Frame: My Life in Words and Pictures*, 2011.

183 Patrick Hamilton, *The West Pier*, 1951 – but set in the early 1920s.

186 Don Airey interview with BBC Wear, 29 October 2014, archived on the BBC website.

187 For Raymond Williams' comments on D H Lawrence see *Culture and Society 1780-1950*, 1958.

ACKNOWLEDGEMENTS

I wouldn't have started without Ian Mole's example and encouragement.

Vanessa has supplemented my own memories with hers, and has been a constant source of encouragement – and honest criticism.

My friend Alan Hooper read the first draft with the same care and insight that he brought to my previous book, on modern British history and politics. He satisfied my enthusiasm for Ackerley with an entertaining biography and a collection of his letters. He loaned me Leonard Woolf's *Growing*, his first volume of autobiography published in 1960, which helped to clarify my thoughts on generations, and Robert Macfarlane's *The Old Ways*, which showed that I wasn't the first author to find inspiration in the stretch of the Icknield Way running west from Letchworth.

I pay tribute to another friend, Andrew Nicholas, who was struck down by Covid while I was working on the book. He loaned me books on the Battle of the Atlantic which clarified my understanding of U-Boat tactics. I'm glad he had the chance to read early versions of Chapters 3 and 8.

I also acknowledge help from members of my wider family. My uncle Ivor's daughter (my cousin) Shirley Moses told me how he ended his days. My aunt Peggie's grand-daughter (my second cousin) Ruth Selwyn-Crome supplied information about her grandmother and her family.

Friends from schooldays also helped. John Tumman from the Bede clarified my understanding of the growth of Sunderland and the railways connecting the port to local collieries. Pat Burn from Hill View told me who played in Green Onions, one of the local groups from the 1960s

I owe special thanks to two boyhood companions Christopher Pike and David Parnaby who confirmed my recollections and added some of their own. Ian Wall, a good friend since childhood, confirmed the accuracy of the numerous episodes in which he figures while deprecating my concern with the past and my obsession with girls. I thought all teenage lads were like me.

Thanks also to other friends for encouraging comments on the first draft; and to members of Facebook groups who unwittingly assisted my research by answering questions and posting photographs. As ever, faults and errors – and embarrassing infelicities – are mine.

I'm grateful to the families of Pauline Mullen and Graham Mole for permission to dedicate my book to their memory.

I sought permission from copyright holders to quote from 'He's a Rebel' written by Gene Pitney, 'Learning the Game' by Buddy Holly, and 'The In Crowd' by Billy Page, but received no response.

ABOUT THE AUTHOR

Michael was born in South Shields in 1949 and moved to Sunderland in 1953. He attended Bede Grammar School between 1960 and 1967. He studied History at Sussex University and graduated in 1970. He spent 21 years as a civil servant, working mainly in Whitehall, before leaving in 1995 to work as a university lecturer. For 26 years he taught at several universities, running courses in Politics and Public Policy, History, Sociology and International Relations, before retiring in 2021. He has lived in Letchworth for 33 years. He has two grown-up sons, David and Henry, both living in London. He has a younger sister, Vanessa, living in Windsor. In 2000 he published a book on modern British politics. He began the present book during lockdown in 2020. It describes the lives of Michael's grandparents and parents and his own life until 18 when he left Sunderland for university. An exasperated manager once described him as a born rebel. He took it as a compliment.